DK EYEWITNESS

T0066958

TOP **10**
LOS ANGELES

Top 10 Los Angeles Highlights

The Top 10 of Everything

CONTENTS

Los Angeles Area by Area

Streetsmart

Within each Top 10 list in this book, no hierarchy of quality or popularity is implied. All 10 are, in the editor's opinion, of roughly equal merit.
  Throughout this book, floors are referred to in accordance with American usage; i.e., the "first floor" is at ground level.

Title page, front cover and spine
Spectacular view of Los Angeles from the iconic Hollywood Sign
Back cover, clockwise from top left
Downtown Los Angeles; sunset at Santa Monica Pier; Hollywood Walk of Fame; Hollywood Sign; aerial view of Huntington Pier

The rate at which the world is changing is constantly keeping the DK Eyewitness team on our toes. While we've worked hard to ensure that this edition of Los Angeles is accurate and up-to-date, we know that opening hours alter, standards shift, prices fluctuate, places close and new ones pop up in their stead. So, if you notice we've got something wrong or left something out, we want to hear about it. Please get in touch at **travelguides@dk.com**

Welcome to
Los Angeles

Hollywood's star-laden streets. World-class museums. Shopping on Rodeo Drive. Road trips along the sweeping Pacific Coast Highway. Surfers riding the perfect wave. The image of Los Angeles is as enticing as it's ever been. With DK Eyewitness Top 10 Los Angeles, the city is yours to explore.

Long mythologized as the City of Dreams, LA has an enduring movie-star image – epitomized by the city's iconic Hollywood sign and wealth of celebrity residents. Famous movies have been filmed all around this city and many iconic backdrops have changed little since their time on the big screen. But beneath this fantastical layer lies a vibrant and multicultural city. Stroll down any street and you can hear a dozen different languages and sample food from all over the world. Head to Koreatown for some of the city's best BBQ joints or indulge in delicious Mexican cuisine in the **Downtown** area.

This is a city that dictates culture to the world. Outstanding museums such as the **Getty Center**, the **Los Angeles County Museum of Art (LACMA)**, and **The Huntington** showcase some of the world's best art. Architecture abounds, with striking contemporary buildings rising from the city center streets and Craftsman-era houses sitting pretty in **Pasadena**. Meanwhile, areas such as **Venice Beach** have seen free-spirited creativity blending with tech innovation.

Whether you're visiting for a weekend or a week, our Top 10 guide brings together the best of everything that Los Angeles has to offer, from iconic places such as **Hollywood** to the amazing **Disneyland® Resort**. The guide has useful tips throughout, from seeking out what's free to getting off the beaten path, plus ten easy-to-follow itineraries designed to tie together a clutch of sights in a short space of time. Add inspiring photography and detailed maps, and you've got the essential pocket-sized travel companion. **Enjoy the book, and enjoy Los Angeles**.

Clockwise from top: **Los Angeles skyline, Walt Disney Concert Hall, North Vista at The Huntington, Rodeo Drive sign, A Los Angeles beach with colorful beach houses, West Coaster at Santa Monica Pier, Street performer on Hollywood's Walk of Fame**

Exploring Los Angeles

From the pier of Santa Monica overlooking the Pacific to the star-lined streets of Hollywood, this vast area presents a carousel of activities. Angelenos excel in having fun, whether it's at the beaches, the museums, or the world-famous amusement parks. These two- and four-day itineraries will help you make the most of your time in Los Angeles.

The Hollywood Sign makes for an iconic sight high on the hillside above the city.

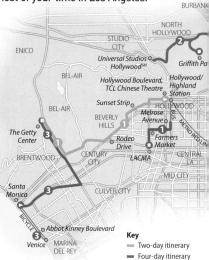

Key
— Two-day itinerary
— Four-day itinerary

Two Days in Los Angeles

Day ❶
MORNING
Start the day on **Historic Hollywood Boulevard** (see pp12–13), at the **TCL Chinese Theatre** (see p63), where you can step among the footprints of the stars. From the Ovation Hollywood, spot the famous **Hollywood Sign** (see p99). Then drive past the sights of **Sunset Strip** (see pp14–15). Continue into Beverly Hills for lunch on **Rodeo Drive** (see p68).

AFTERNOON
Head to **The Getty Center** (see pp16–19), a masterpiece of the LA community – wandering through the Impressionist room or the gardens, while taking in the fabulous views of the coastline and hills.

Day ❷
MORNING
Enjoy breakfast at **Marston's** (see p97) in Pasadena before heading over to **The Huntington** (see pp28–31). Pick a couple of gardens to focus on – like the Desert Garden or Rose Garden – and then step into the Art Museum to view the masterpieces on display.

AFTERNOON
Take the Metro to Union Station, Downtown. Cross the street to **El Pueblo de Los Angeles** (see pp24–25) and have lunch on Olvera Street. From Alameda Street, take the DASH B bus to the striking **Cathedral of Our Lady of Angels** (see p78). Walk down South Grand Avenue to see the **Walt Disney Concert Hall** (see p78), **MOCA** (see p78), and **The Broad** museum (see p80).

Downtown

Hollywood/Highland
8 miles (13 km)

Pasadena
12 miles
(20 km)

Cathedral of Our
Lady of the Angels

Olvera St

DASH B BUS

Union
Station

Walt Disney
Concert Hall

The Broad

El Pueblo de
Los Angeles

MOCA

Grand
Central Market

0 meters   500
0 yards   500

PASADENA

GLENDALE

Marston's
Del Mar Station

METRO GOLD LINE

The Huntington

LOS ANGELES
COUNTY

ALHAMBRA

SILVER
LAKE

ECHO
PARK

MONTECITO
HEIGHTS

see Downtown
inset

0 km   3

0 miles   3

DOWNTOWN

Disneyland and
California Adventure
30 miles (48 km)

Four Days in Los Angeles

Day ❶

MORNING

After breakfast at Downtown's **Grand Central Market** (see p79), cross Broadway and admire the **Bradbury Building** (see p49). Walk over to South Grand Avenue to admire **The Broad** museum (see p80) and the **Walt Disney Concert Hall** (see p78). Take DASH B bus to **El Pueblo de Los Angeles** (see pp24–25) and explore LA's early history. From Union Station, take the Metro to Hollywood/Highland Station.

AFTERNOON

Try a little star-gazing on **Historic Hollywood Boulevard** (see pp12–13) before taking a bus or taxi down to **Melrose Avenue** (see p68) for shopping. Have lunch here or at the **Farmers Market** (see p107) on Fairfax Avenue. Enjoy some of LA's finest art and culture over at **LACMA** (see pp20–23), a few blocks away.

Day ❷

MORNING

Spend the morning among the roses at **The Huntington** (see pp28–31) before driving over to **Universal Studios Hollywood**ˢᴹ (see pp32–3).

AFTERNOON

Focus on the most popular attractions, such as the famed Wizarding World of Harry Potter Studio tour, and Jurassic World: The Ride. Then head over to **Griffith Park** (see pp34–5).

Day ❸

MORNING

Pedal a rental bicycle from Santa Monica to Venice along the famous **Venice Boardwalk** (see p122). Next, snack like a local at **Venice Ale House** (see p124). Return along **Abbot Kinney Boulevard** and **Main Street** (see p69).

AFTERNOON

Enjoy a blissful afternoon at **The Getty Center** (see pp16–19).

Day ❹

MORNING

Disneyland® **Resort** and **California Adventure**® (see pp36–41) really require a full day. Buy a Park Hopper ticket that allows entry into both parks. Spend the morning on the rides at Disneyland®.

AFTERNOON

Shift over to California Adventure® by late afternoon and be sure to stay for the spectacular World of Color display at night.

Venice Boardwalk makes for an exciting cycling spot.

Top 10 Los Angeles Highlights

The impressive auditorium
at the TCL Chinese Theatre

🔟 Los Angeles Highlights

The myth, the velocity, the edginess in creative and technological fields – this is Los Angeles. In just over 200 years, LA has grown from a dusty Spanish outpost into one of the world's largest and most complex cities offering top venues for everything from archaeology and the arts to food. The birthplace of Mickey Mouse and Hollywood, LA has shaped the imaginations of millions.

1 Historic Hollywood Boulevard
The boulevard that gave birth to the movie industry is still associated with the stars, even if the only ones around today are embedded in the sidewalk (see pp12–13).

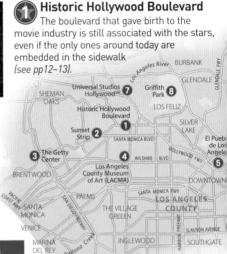

2 Sunset Strip
The heady mix of hip restaurants, nightclubs, and bars along the city's entertainment mile attracts legions of the young and the trendy (see pp14–15).

3 The Getty Center
This striking hilltop complex, which is free to visit and promises stunning views, is a must for fans of European art (see pp16–19).

4 Los Angeles County Museum of Art (LACMA)
One of America's largest art museums, LACMA offers a survey of art from prehistoric times to the present (see pp20–23).

5 El Pueblo de Los Angeles
This historic district preserves LA's oldest buildings, celebrating its Mexican past with stores, restaurants, and festivals (see pp24–5).

6 The Huntington

One of LA's great cultural treasures invites visitors to experience its fine paintings, rare manuscripts, and gorgeous gardens (see pp28–31).

7 Universal Studios Hollywood℠

A day at Universal involves high-tech thrill rides, live action shows, and special-effects extravaganzas. The Studio Tour takes visitors to the backlot of the working movie studio (see pp32–3).

8 Griffith Park

One of the largest city parks in the US, Griffith Park offers a combination of rugged wilderness and diversions such as museums and an observatory (see pp34–5). The Hollywood Sign is here too.

9 Disneyland® Resort

As timeless as Mickey Mouse himself, the original Disney park hasn't lost its magic more than 70 years after it opened (see pp36–41).

10 Catalina Island

This island is a quick and easy getaway. Its considerable charms include crystal-clear waters, miles of undeveloped back country, and a sense of being far away from the bustle of big city LA (see pp42–3).

TOP 10 ⭐ Historic Hollywood Boulevard

Hollywood Boulevard, home of the Walk of Fame, has always been synonymous with the glamour of moviemaking, especially in the 1920s and 1930s. After a period of decline in the 1970s, the heart of Tinseltown cleaned up its act with some major revitalization – the old movie palaces received facelifts, the Ovation Hollywood complex became a major draw, and the Oscars began to be hosted at the Dolby Theatre.

1 Walk of Fame

Elvis, Lassie, and over 2,700 other celebs have been immortalized with terrazzo and brass stars in the sidewalk **(below)**. A few "special" stars, such as those for the Apollo 11 astronauts, are also installed nearby.

3 TCL Chinese Theatre

The world's most famous movie theater **(above)** opened in 1927 *(see p63)* with a screening of Cecil B. DeMille's *King of Kings*. About 200 stars have left their hand- and foot-prints here, and Betty Grable even left prints of her famous legs.

5 The Hollywood Roosevelt

Douglas Fairbanks Sr. presided over the first Academy Awards at this historic hotel **(below)** in 1929, and Marilyn Monroe shot her first commercial by the pool *(see p145)*, later adorned with blue squiggles by the artist David Hockney.

2 Musso & Frank Grill

During Hollywood's Golden Years, this was the haunt *(see p103)* of stars such as Clark Gable and the Marx Brothers. Opened in 1919, it is the oldest restaurant in Hollywood and much of its classic interior still remains unchanged.

4 Pantages Theatre

The grande dame of Tinseltown theaters *(see p64)* sparkles once again in all its restored Art Deco glory. The lobby leads to the magnificent auditorium with its elaborate ceiling. It now hosts blockbuster Broadway shows.

8 Ovation Hollywood

This cornerstone of Hollywood revitalization and mega-entertainment complex **(left)** combines shops, restaurants, night clubs, movie theaters, a hotel, and the 3,400-seat Dolby Theatre *(see p65)*, home of the Oscars.

A STAR FOR THE STARS

A star on the Walk of Fame requires the prior approval of a screening committee appointed by the Hollywood Chamber of Commerce. Of the 200 applications received every year, only 10 per cent get the nod – and the privilege to pay the $40,000 fee for installation and main-tenance. Studios – and sometimes fan clubs – usually foot the bill. Induction ceremonies are held once or twice a month and are open to the public. Check out www.walkoffame.com to see who's up next.

NEED TO KNOW

MAP P2 ■ Stretches from La Brea Blvd to Vine St

Walk of Fame: Hollywood Blvd between Gower St & La Brea Ave, and Vine St between Yucca Ave & Sunset Blvd

Ovation Hollywood: 6801 Hollywood Blvd

Capitol Records Tower: 1750 N Vine St

Hollywood Museum: 1660 Highland Ave

■ Head to Cookie Dough Dreams in Ovation Hollywood to try handmade cookie dough that you can eat raw.

■ Get off the B Line on Hollywood Boulevard at either Highland or Vine to reach the Walk of Fame.

Map of Historic Hollywood Boulevard

6 The Egyptian Theatre

Owned by Netflix since 2020, this landmark theater *(see p62)* is the birthplace of the "Hollywood premiere".

7 Capitol Records Tower

Still the headquarters of Capitol Records, the world's first circular office building looks like a pile of records with a stylus blinking out "Hollywood" in Morse code.

9 Hollywood Museum

The historic Art Deco Max Factor building showcases a hundred years of film costumes, props, and memorabilia.

10 El Capitan Theatre

The strikingly ornate El Capitan *(see p63)* was Hollywood's first live theater and began screening films in 1941. Today, it is a Disney first-run movie theater.

⭐ Sunset Strip

Sunset Strip has been a haven of hedonism since Prohibition days. Wedged between Hollywood and Beverly Hills, this 1.7 miles (2.7 km) of the Sunset Boulevard is crammed with buzzing nightclubs, hip rock venues, and fashionable boutiques. During Hollywood's Glamour Age (1930–50), the stars trysted at the Chateau Marmont, partied at Trocadero, and talked shop at Schwab's Pharmacy. Today's hot spots rub shoulders with some historical landmarks.

1 Sunset Plaza

This two-block stretch is lined with European-style restaurants and designer shops teeming with fashionable crowds. Its appeal with celebrities makes it prime territory for star-spotting.

3 Giant Billboards

A testimony to the Strip's unabashed commercialism, these mega-sized billboards **(right)** promote movies, records, products, and even individual stars.

2 Andaz West Hollywood

Formerly known as the "Riot Hyatt," this hotel **(above)** is part of rock history as party central for British bands in the 1960s and 1970s. Led Zeppelin cruised down the halls on motorcycles.

Map of Sunset Strip

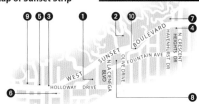

6 The Viper Room

Actor River Phoenix died outside this *(see p112)* club **(left)**. Few remember its earlier incarnation as the Melody Room, a favorite with Bugsy Siegel and his mobster pals.

SUNSET BOULEVARD

Sunset Strip takes up only a small portion of the 25-mile (40-km) Sunset Boulevard. Following the path of an old cattle trail, this major cross-town artery is a microcosm of the cultural, ethnic, and social cauldron that is LA. Starting at El Pueblo in Downtown, it travels west through different neighborhoods, before spilling into the Pacific.

8 Roxy Theatre

This historic venue has been launching the careers of musicians and singer-songwriters for 50 years. Everyone from Neil Young to Mötley Crue have played on its stage.

9 Rainbow Bar & Grill

This rock'n'roll bar has long been popular with musicians such as Mötley Crüe and Rod Stewart. When it was still the Villa Nova restaurant, Marilyn Monroe met Joe DiMaggio on a blind date here.

4 Site of Schwab's Pharmacy

In the 1930s and 1940s, Schwab's Pharmacy was a hip hangout frequented by Charlie Chaplin and James Dean. It was torn down in 1988.

5 Whisky a Go-Go

A Strip fixture since 1963, the Whisky *(see p112)* gave the world go-go dancing and The Doors, its house band in 1966. Other stars such as Jimi Hendrix and Janis Joplin also played here.

7 Chateau Marmont

This 1927 hotel **(below)**, has hosted celebrities such as Humphrey Bogart and Mick Jagger. Annie Leibovitz, Dorothy Parker, and Jane Fonda have spent time living here while they worked on different Hollywood projects.

10 Sunset Tower Hotel

This Art Deco gem *(see p146)*, formerly known as the Argyle, opened in 1931 and has been the home of many a star. Its bar remains a hot address today.

TOP 10 ★ The Getty Center

A spectacular art collection, superb architecture, and lovely gardens combine with a hilltop location to create one of LA's finest cultural destinations. Designed by Richard Meier, the Getty Center opened in December 1997 after 14 years of planning and construction. It unites the entities of the Getty Trust created by oil tycoon J. Paul Getty (1892–1976), including research and conservation institutes. At its core is the museum, with its exquisite European art from illuminated manuscripts to contemporary photography.

1 Cabinet on Stand
Celebrating the triumphs of French king Louis XIV, this cabinet **(right)** has been attributed to André-Charles Boulle (1642–1732). The design features several materials, including pewter and tortoiseshell.

2 The Adoration of the Magi
In this Renaissance masterpiece, Andrea Mantegna (c1431–1506) emulates ancient Roman reliefs to achieve an intimacy between subjects. The three kings represent Europe, Asia, and Africa.

3 Irises
Dutchman Vincent van Gogh (1853–90) painted this detailed work **(left)** in the last year of his life in a mental asylum. The intense color and energetic composition borrow from Gauguin and Japanese printmaker Hokusai.

7 The Abduction of Europa

Rembrandt (1606–69) found great inspiration in Ovid's *Metamorphoses*. This work captures Jupiter, disguised as a white bull, spiriting away the princess Europa across the oceans.

8 Self-Portrait, Yawning

Decreux's (1735–1802) dynamic presentation of himself while letting out a great yawn was part of his study of physiology and emotion. The painter created dozens of exaggerated self-portraits.

4 Young Italian Woman at a Table

This emotionally charged painting **(above)** by Cézanne (1839–1906) shows off his great versatility and technical ability.

5 Wheatstacks, Snow Effect, Morning

This is one of 30 works that Monet (1840–1926) painted between 1890 and 1891. Set against a soft sky and faintly visible houses, the wheatstacks form a solid, imposing presence in the picture.

6 Albert Cahen d'Anvers

Pierre-Auguste Renoir painted this portrait of composer Cahen d'Anvers in 1881 while deciding to take up commissioned portraiture professionally.

GETTY VILLA

In a separate location on the Pacific Coast Highway, this museum and educational center is set in a re-creation of an ancient Roman country house and houses over 44,000 Greek, Roman, and Etruscan antiquities dating from 6,500 BCE to 400 CE. Among the 1,200 items on display are sculptures, everyday artifacts, and treasures such as Cycladic figures. Five of the museum's 28 galleries are devoted to changing exhibitions.

9 Modern Rome, Campo Vaccino

Joseph Turner's view of Rome from the Capitoline Hill **(above)** is the last of his Roman paintings. It shows why this English artist (1775–1851) was celebrated as the "painter of light".

10 Christ's Entry into Brussels in 1889

Belgian James Ensor's (1860–1949) painting is one of the most controversial works of the 19th century. The grotesque scene reflects the artist's uneasiness with society.

NEED TO KNOW

MAP C2

Getty Center: 1200 Getty Center Dr, Brentwood; 310-440-7300; open 10am–5:30pm Tue–Sun (until 8pm Sat); www.getty.edu; parking $20 ($15 after 3pm)

Getty Villa: 17985 Pacific Coast Highway; 310-440-7300; open 10am–5pm Wed–Mon; advance timed ticket required; parking $20 ($15 after 3pm)

■ Picnic in the gardens or courtyard, or buy a light meal at a kiosk or the self-service café.

For gourmet meals, book at The Restaurant.

■ The Getty welcomes kids, with special child-oriented audio guides and a staffed Family Room with games and various hands-on activities.

■ Free architecture and garden tours are offered.

Top 10 Features of the Getty

Water feature in the Central Garden

1 Central Garden
These beautiful – and constantly changing – gardens were designed by visual artist Robert Irwin (b.1928). Wander along tree-lined paths and across a gentle stream to a reflecting pool with floating azaleas and ringed by beautiful specialty gardens.

2 Electric Tram
The Getty experience kicks off with a smooth five-minute ride up the hill from the parking garage to the Arrival Plaza in a driverless, computer-operated tram.

3 Panoramic Views
On clear days, the views from the Getty's hilltop perch are spectacular, especially around sunset. Take in the vastness of LA's labyrinthine streets, the skyscrapers of Downtown, the surrounding Santa Monica Mountains, and the Pacific Ocean.

4 Illuminated Manuscripts
Shown on a rotating basis, the Getty's collection of illuminated manuscripts covers the entire Middle Ages and Renaissance. *The Stammheim Missal* (1120) from Germany is among the most prized.

The Stammheim Missal

5 Drawings
Highlights of this collection, dating from the 14th to the 19th centuries, include Albrecht Dürer's exquisite *The Stag Beetle* (1505) and da Vinci's *Studies for the Christ Child with Lamb* (c.1503–6).

6 Shopping and Dining
There are plenty of options for a day-long visit, including the Museum Store and shops devoted to photography, and the latest exhibits. For refreshments, try the restaurant, café, coffee carts, or bring your own gourmet picnic.

7 Decorative Arts
The Getty's famous collection of French decorative art and furniture from the 17th and 18th centuries is displayed in a series of period rooms. The paneled Régence salon from 1710 is a must-see.

8 Photography
Known for its images from the early 1840s, the collection concentrates on work by European and American artists. Man Ray's *Tears* is among the most famous pieces.

9 European Painting
Paintings from the Italian Renaissance and Baroque periods, as well as French Impressionism, are particularly well represented.

10 Outdoor Sculpture
Works by many of the 20th century's greatest sculptors are displayed throughout the grounds. The sculptures, including work by Henry Moore, Alberto Giacometti, and Joan Miró, were donated by the late producer Ray Stark and his wife, Fran.

THE ARCHITECTURE

Roosting on its hilltop site on the edge of the Santa Monica Mountains, the Getty Center is an imposing presence, far removed from city noise and bustle. An amazing feat of architecture and engineering, it was designed by New York-based Modernist Richard Meier (b 1934), an internationally acclaimed architect who also drafted the Paley Center for Media in Beverly Hills *(see p116)*. For the Getty, Meier arranged the main buildings along two natural ridges connected by creative landscaping. Curvilinear elements, such as in the Museum Entrance Hall, combine with angular structures to create an effect of fluidity and openness. This is further enhanced by the use of travertine, a honey-colored, fossil-textured stone quarried in Italy that covers most buildings.

TOP 10
BUILDING STATISTICS

1 Campus size: 24 acres (10 ha)

2 Campus altitude: 900 ft (275 m)

3 Cost: $1 billion

4 Cubic yards (of earth) moved: 1.5 million

5 Travertine used: 16,000 tons

6 Weight of each travertine block: 250 lb (113 kg)

7 Enameled aluminum panels: 40,000

8 Exterior glass: 164,650 sq ft (15,296 sq m)

9 Number of doors: 3,200

10 Length of tram ride: 0.75 miles (1.2 km)

The Getty's columns and vast scale give it the feel of a modern – and thoroughly American – Acropolis.

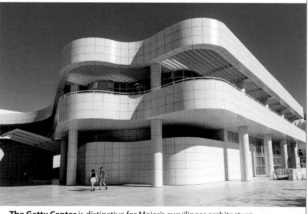

The Getty Center is distinctive for Meier's curvilinear architecture.

🔟⭐ Los Angeles County Museum of Art (LACMA)

The largest art museum in the western US, Los Angeles County Museum of Art was founded in 1910 and moved to its present home in 1965. Its vast collection features art from Europe, the Americas, Asia, and the Middle East. There is a lively schedule of concerts, lectures, and film screenings, too. In 2010, the Resnick Pavilion was added, a vast open-plan space designed by Renzo Piano that houses rotating exhibitions.

2 Ancient and Islamic Art

LACMA's Art of the Ancient World collection **(left)** spans more than 4,000 years and features horse trappings, stone reliefs, and pottery. The collection also includes the Islamic Art display, which is renowned for its wide range of art forms.

5 Photography and Prints and Drawings

LACMA's photography collection focuses on images produced in the last 60 years, whereas the Prints and Drawings collection includes art from the 15th century to the present day.

1 Japanese Art

The Pavilion for Japanese Art is the only building in the US devoted to Japanese art. It is closed for retrofitting and will reopen in 2024.

3 American Art

This collection offers a survey of American art from the 1700s to the 1940s. Among the highlights are works by late 19th-century figurative artists such as Winslow Homer. Other works include paintings by George Bellows and Mary Cassatt, specifically *Mother About to Wash her Sleepy Child*.

4 European Painting and Sculpture

A collection of works **(below)** by Flemish and Dutch masters and French Impressionists, including Monet's *In the Woods at Giverny*.

COLLECTION GUIDE

The renovated LACMA campus, opening in late 2024, will replace four of the seven older buildings. The David Geffen Galleries are expected to offer more indoor space for the permanent collection, an education center, and outdoor plazas. Meanwhile, exhibitions are being held at BCAM (Broad Contemporary Art Museum) and the Resnick Pavilion. These feature a rotating display of artworks from the museum's permanent collection.

6 South and Southeast Asian Art

This collection is one of the world's finest, with sculpture, watercolors, illustrated manuscripts, ritual art, and coins from the 11th to the 20th century. Among the highlights are Indian art and sculpture **(left)**.

9 Latin American Art

This collection features ancient American, Spanish colonial, contemporary, and modern works. Key pieces range from Mayan works and art by, Orozco, Wifredo Lam, and Torres-Garcia.

Visitors admiring the paintings at LACMA

7 Decorative Arts and Design

This collection features European and American decorative design from the Middle Ages to the present. It includes The Palevsky Arts and Crafts collection.

8 Chinese and Korean Art

The largest collection of Korean art outside of South Korea has work from the 5th to the 20th century. Chinese galleries include ceramics, beautiful paintings, and bronzes.

10 Modern and Contemporary Art

Matisse, Picasso, and Magritte are among the artists represented in the Modern Art collection that spans from 1945 to the present day, and ranges from paintings to video installations.

NEED TO KNOW

MAP N6 ▪ 5905 Wilshire Blvd, Midtown ▪ 323-857-6000 ▪ www.lacma.org

Open 11am–6pm Mon, Tue, & Thu, 11am–8pm Fri, 10am–7pm Sat & Sun

Adm adults $25; seniors & students $21; $10 for under 17s; free for under 2s; extra charge for special exhibits

▪ The LACMA houses rotating exhibitions – not all items listed are guaranteed to be on display.

▪ Free films, Sunday family days, workshops, and gallery tours are offered at different times of the year. Check website.

▪ Upgrades to the museum are ongoing. Check www.buildinglacma.org.

Top 10 LACMA Masterpieces

1 Portrait of Mrs Edward L. Davis and Her Son, Livingston Davis
John Singer Sargent (1856–1925) was a gifted East Coast society portrait painter. This 1890 work blends loose brushwork (the boy) with stark realism (his mother).

2 Standing Warrior
Standing about 3-ft (1-m) tall, this figure of a king or warrior is the largest-known effigy from western Mexico. It dates from between 200 BCE and 300 CE.

3 Eagle-Headed Deity
Ancient Syrian palaces were often decorated with intricately carved-stone slabs. This one depicts a deity in the process of fertilizing a tree by scattering pollen from a pail.

Thangka depicting Yama and Yami

5 Yama and Yami
At nearly 2.4-m (8-ft) high, this is one of the largest Tibetan *thangka* paintings outside Tibet. It dates from the late 17th to early 18th century and has undergone extensive restoration.

6 Untitled Improvisation III
A pioneer of pure abstract painting, Russian-born Wassily Kandinsky (1866–1944) imbued his canvasses with spirituality expressed through shapes and bold colors, as in this 1914 work.

7 Untitled (S.027, Hanging, Six-and-a-Half Open Hyperbolic Shapes that Penetrate Each Other)
Japanese American sculptor Ruth Asawa (1926–2013) is renowned for her kinetic wire sculptures. This piece is more than 2.4-m (8-ft) tall.

8 Mulholland Drive
LA-based British artist David Hockney (b1937) created many panoramic paintings such as this brightly

The Magdalen with the Smoking Flame

4 The Magdalen with the Smoking Flame
French Baroque artist Georges de La Tour (1593–1652) employs deep contrasts between light and shadow to depict his subject with great intimacy and realism.

colored and dynamically composed 1980 work, which shows the famous LA road linking the artist's house and studio.

⑨ Shiva as the Lord of Dance

This exquisite sculpture from the 11th century portrays the Hindu god Shiva as the source of cosmic dance, which defines the universe as

Shiva as the Lord of Dance

a continuous cycle of creation, preservation, and destruction.

⑩ Urban Light

The American sculpture and installation artist Chris Burden (1946–2015) arranged 202 vintage cast-iron street lamps that once resided on the streets of LA into an elegant forest of light and magic that comes to life at sunset.

THE MIRACLE MILE

LACMA sits on a particularly interesting and historic stretch of Wilshire Boulevard. The so-called "Miracle Mile" was the city's first shopping district outside of Downtown and the first ever designed with easy access for the motorized shopper. The man behind this vision was developer A. W. Ross, who, in 1921, bought 18 acres (7 ha) of land between La Brea Boulevard and Fairfax Avenue with the lofty goal of turning it into a "Fifth Avenue of the West." His plan was a wild success, as department stores and upscale retail establishments quickly moved in, but it also marked the beginning of LA's decentralization. By the 1960s, however, a new innovation – the shopping mall – spelled the end of the "miracle." Although a shadow of its former self, the Miracle Mile has been revitalized to some extent, with galleries, restaurants, and music venues attracting visitors. A few of the Art Deco buildings have survived and are now on the National Register of Historic Places.

TOP 10 OF ART DECO ON THE MIRACLE MILE

1 Saban Building (1940): Wilshire at Fairfax Ave

2 El Rey Theater (1928): 5517 Wilshire Blvd

3 Desmonds Department Store Building (1929): 5514 Wilshire Blvd

4 Commercial Building (1927): 5464 Wilshire Blvd

5 Roman's Food Mart (1935): 5413 Wilshire Blvd

6 Chandler's Shoe Store (1938): Wilshire at Cloverdale Ave

7 Dominguez-Wilshire Blvd (1930): 5410 Wilshire Blvd

8 The Dark Room (1938): 5370 Wilshire Blvd

9 Wilson Building (1930): 5217–31 Wilshire Blvd

10 Security Pacific Bank Building (1929): 5209 Wilshire Blvd

Saban building houses the stunning Academy Museum of Motion Pictures.

TOP 10 ⭐ El Pueblo de Los Angeles

This historic district protects LA's oldest structures, all built between 1818 and 1926. It is believed to be close to the site where 44 Mexican men, women, and children established El Pueblo de Los Angeles in the name of the Spanish crown in 1781. It also reflects the heritage of other ethnic groups that arrived later, including Chinese, Italians, and Swiss. As LA grew into a metropolis, businesses relocated and the area plunged into deep decline. Now restored, three of El Pueblo de Los Angeles' 27 structures contain museums.

1 América Tropical

Mexican artist David Alfaro Siqueiros's controversial 1932 mural is a visceral allegory about the exploitation of Mexican workers.

2 Blessing of the Animals

Italian-American artist Leo Politi's endearing 1978 mural shows the tradition of asking the Catholic church to bless livestock with good health and productivity. Celebrations take place in the Old Plaza each year.

THE MOTHER OF OLVERA STREET

Had it not been for Christine Sterling (1881–1963), an LA socialite-turned-civic activist, the El Pueblo de Los Angeles area may have been completely different. Dismayed by the decline of LA's oldest neighborhood, Sterling launched a campaign to save it in 1926, backed by *LA Times* publisher Harry Chandler and others. In April 1930, Olvera Street was reincarnated as a busy Mexican market. The Avila Adobe contains an exhibit on her triumph.

3 Old Plaza

Music, dancing, and fun fills the Old Plaza during lively fiestas. It has sculptures of King Carlos III of Spain (1716–88) and Felipe de Neve (1724–84), and a plaque listing the original settlers honors LA's founders.

5 Sepulveda House

Eloisa Sepulveda built this 22-room Victorian house in 1887 as her home, a hotel, and two stores. It now serves as El Pueblo's Visitor and Orientation Center.

Olvera Street 4

Known locally as La Placita Olvera, this busy, brick-paved lane has been a Mexican marketplace (right) since 1930. Wander past and try some tacos or *tortas*.

6 Pico House

Pio Pico, the last Mexican governor of California, built this grand edifice **(above)** in 1870. It was LA's first three-story structure and once a hotel.

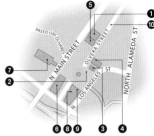

Map of El Pueblo de Los Angeles

9 Old Plaza Firehouse

This two-story brick building is a must-see. Firehouse No.1 with its all-volunteer crew and horse-drawn equipment was operational until 1897. Check out a small exhibit of memorabilia.

10 Avila Adobe

LA's oldest surviving house **(below)**, built by mayor Don Francisco Avila in 1818, went through several incarnations as a military headquarters and boarding house. Today, it is a historic house museum.

7 Plaza Catholic Church

Worshipers have gathered in LA's oldest church **(above)** since 1822. The original was rebuilt in 1861. Features include the painted ceiling and the main altar framed in gold leaf.

8 Chinese American Museum

The Chinese first settled here in the late 19th century. This museum, housed in the 1890s Garnier Building, traces the community's history.

NEED TO KNOW

MAP W3–4

El Pueblo Visitor Center: 128 Paseo de la Plaza; 213-485-6855; opening hours vary, call for details; www.elpueblo.lacity.gov

Olvera Street: open 10am–7pm daily (some shops may open earlier and close later)

Avila Adobe: open 9am–4pm Tue–Sun

Old Plaza Firehouse: open 10am–3pm daily

Chinese American Museum: 425 N Los Angeles St; open 10am–3pm Tue–Sun; adm $3

▪ Olvera Street is great for an authentic Mexican meal. Try the popular Casa Golondrina or the casual La Luz del Día.

▪ Volunteer docents offer free guided tours of El Pueblo at 10am, 11am, and noon Thursday to Saturday. Check in next to the firehouse. The visitor center offers self-guided tour pamphlets.

Following pages Chinese Garden at The Huntington

TOP 10 ★ The Huntington

The Huntington Library, Art Museums, and Botanical Gardens form one of those rare places that manages to please the eye, stimulate the mind, and nourish the soul all at the same time. The former estate of railroad and real-estate baron Henry E. Huntington (1850–1927), it consists of a trio of treasures: the art galleries display fine examples of British, French, and American art; The Huntington Library has about seven million rare manuscripts and books, including a Gutenberg Bible; and the Botanical Gardens are a feast of flora in a tranquil park-like setting.

3 Japanese Garden

A place for strolling and quiet contemplation, Huntington's Japanese Garden (**right**) is among the oldest of its kind in the US. Its canyon setting is accented by a waterfall, a shimmering pond filled with *koi* fish and water lilies, and a teahouse.

4 Camellia Garden

Camellias reached the US in the 18th century. With about 1,200 types (in bloom during January and February), this is one of the finest collections.

1 Desert Garden

This garden (**above**), with its clusters of unusual cacti and flowering succulents, has an otherworldly feel. One of the world's largest, it's a study of the ways in which desert plants adapt to survive in harsh, arid conditions.

2 Rose Garden

This romantic garden features nearly 1,200 rose varieties, some of them with a pedigree going back to ancient Greece. The historic 1911 Tea Room here reopened in 2023 after a three-year renovation that added a pavilion for alfresco dining.

5 Chinese Garden

This garden, Liu Fang Yuan, or the Garden of Flowering Fragrance, was inspired by the Chinese tradition of using gardens for scholarly purposes. Pavilions and a teahouse encircle a small lake.

6 North Vista

The palms and statues lining the central lawn of this Baroque garden (**below**) evoke old European palaces. The lawn connects the gallery with a dolphin-studded Italian fountain.

Gutenberg Bible

The Huntington Library's star exhibit, this 1455 Bible **(right)** is one of only 12 surviving copies printed on vellum by Johannes Gutenberg of Mainz, Germany, the inventor of movable type. The colorful chapter headings and decorations were added by hand.

A SHORT GUIDE

Access The Huntington from either Orlando Road or Oxford Road. Both lead to a large parking lot and from there to the entrance pavilion, where you can pick up a free map. While you can "do" The Huntington in an hour or two, it's better to come early and spend the day. No admission fee is required at the 1919 Cafe or Red Car Coffee Shop.

NEED TO KNOW

MAP E2 ■ 1151 Oxford Rd, San Marino near Pasadena ■ 626-405-2100 ■ www.huntington.org

Open 10am–5pm Wed–Mon

Adm adults $25 ($29 Fri–Sun & public hols) seniors and students $21 ($24 Fri–Sun); children 4–11 $13; under 4s free; advance online reservations required; free first Thu of month

■ Picnicking is not permitted in the gardens, but allowed in the Garden Court and patio adjacent to the ticketing area. Visitors can grab a bite to eat at 1919 Cafe, Jade Court Cafe, Red Car Coffee Shop or the Rose Garden Tea Room.

■ Plants from the nursery are available for purchase online during spring season.

Boone Gallery

The Boone Gallery began life in 1911 as Henry Huntington's garage. With columns that echo the Neo-Classical style of the mansion, it is used for temporary exhibitions.

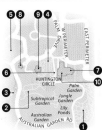

Map of The Huntington

Greene & Greene Exhibit

Charles and Henry Greene, known for their houses and fine furnishings, were pioneers of the early 20th-century Craftsman style *(see p95)*.

Chaucer's "The Canterbury Tales"

This rare 1410 manuscript – known as the "Ellesmere Manuscript" – of English poet Geoffrey Chaucer's most famous work is complete, in fine condition, and filled with luminous illustrations.

Top 10 Huntington Artworks

Pinkie, completed in 1794

Huntington Art Gallery First Floor Plan

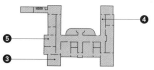

Huntington Art Gallery Second Floor Plan

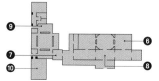

The Scott Galleries of American Art First Floor Plan

1 Pinkie
Thomas Lawrence (1769–1830) painted Sarah Barrett Moulton, nicknamed "Pinkie," aged 11, in a refreshingly direct and lively manner. She died soon after the painting was completed, possibly of consumption.

2 The Blue Boy
Thomas Gainsborough (1727–88) is one of the most acclaimed British society portrait painters. This famous 1770 painting shows his friend Jonathan Buttall in costume.

3 View on the Stour near Dedham
Romantic landscape painter John Constable (1776–1837) adopted a lyrical approach to depicting nature. His emphasis on sky, light, and other intangible qualities influenced other artists, including the Impressionists.

4 Virgin and Child
A master of early Flemish painting, Rogier van der Weyden (c1400–64) infused his works with emotional intensity, evident here in the Virgin's face and hands.

5 The Grand Canal, Venice
This 1837 painting is a fine example of the translucency typical of the works of J. M. W. Turner (1775–1851). The tiny person in the lower right corner is Shylock from the play *The Merchant of Venice.*

The Long Leg, painted in c 1930

6 The Long Leg
The solitude and anonymity of human existence is a recurring theme in the paintings of Edward Hopper (1882–1967), a leading 20th-century American Realist. Here, these sentiments of loneliness are expressed in a famous sailing scene.

7 Chimborazo
A trip to Ecuador inspired this painting by 19th-century American landscape artist, Frederic Church (1826–1900). Church took creative license when compressing the mountains, desert, and jungle into a single image (1864).

8 Breakfast in Bed
Pennsylvania-born Mary Cassatt (1844–1926) moved to Paris in 1873, where she befriended Edgar Degas and fell under the spell of Impressionism. The subject of mother and child was a favorite.

9 The Western Brothers
John Singleton Copley (1738–1815) was born in Colonial Boston and moved to England just before 1776. This 1783 double portrait is characterized by flowing strokes and strong facial expressions.

10 The Robinson Dining Room
This re-created dining room exemplifies the innovative genius of the brothers Charles and Henry Greene. Designed between 1905 and 1907, it contains original furniture and an amazing chandelier.

HENRY HUNTINGTON'S RED CARS

Henry E. Huntington made his vast fortune by marrying real-estate speculation with public transportation. The largest landowner in Southern California, he established the Pacific Electric Railway in 1901, primarily to get people out to the far-flung new suburbs he was developing. Soon Huntington's fleet of interurban red trolleys – dubbed the "Red Cars" – became the world's largest electric-transit system, linking communities across Southern California. By the time he sold most of his holdings to the Southern Pacific Railroad in 1910, the population of LA had tripled to around 310,000. "The last trolley" made its farewell voyage in 1961, though a section of the Red Car line was restored in San Pedro and the Red Cars ran once more between 2003–2015.

A model of the popular Red Car trolleys is one of the highlights of The Huntington collection.

TOP 10 RED CARS FACTS AND STATS

1 Covered four counties
2 Linked 50 communities
3 First ride: 1901
4 Last ride: 1961
5 Track: 1,150 miles (1,850 km)
6 Fleet: 900 cars at peak
7 Passengers: 109 million in 1944 (peak year)
8 Fare: a penny a mile
9 Top speed: 40–50 mph (60–80 km/h)
10 Car length: 50 ft (15 m)

TOP 10 ⭐ Universal Studios Hollywood^{SM}

The world's largest movie and television studio sprang from the imagination of cinema pioneer Carl Laemmle. In 1915, he bought a former chicken ranch, brought in cameras, lights, and actors, and started making silent films. The theme park began taking shape in 1964. Today, Universal Studios Hollywood^{SM} gets more visitors (about 8.5 million a year) than any other attraction in LA County.

① King Kong
The King Kong 360 3-D is the first theme park attraction created by Peter Jackson, who directed the Oscar-winning 2005 film upon which it is based. Guests enter into a world where the film and tram are tied into a simulator that creates a titanic struggle between the 30-ft (9.1-m) tall gorilla and gigantic dinosaurs **(above)**. It is billed as "the largest, most intense 3-D experience on the planet."

② CityWalk
A lively carnival atmosphere reigns along this studio-adjacent promenade with its mix of restaurants, shops, neon signs, and entertainment venues.

③ Studio Tour
For a look at movie-making, this 60-minute narrated tram tour **(right)** of the actual working studio is a must. Cruise past 35 soundstages to the vast backlot and outdoor sets.

④ The Simpsons Ride™
Join the Simpsons in the Krustyland theme park as they try to save Bart from Sideshow Bob. The characters are all voiced by the original actors.

5 Jurassic World – The Ride

An upgrade to the previous ride, this **(above)** is part expedition and part thrilling water ride based on the film franchise.

8 DreamWorks Theatre Featuring Kung Fu Panda

This multi-sensory experience uses ground-breaking interior projection mapping, 360 degree surround sound, and a multitude of special effects on a trip with Master Po and his entourage.

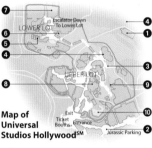

Map of Universal Studios Hollywood^{SM}

6 Revenge of The Mummy^{SM} – The Ride

The park's first ever roller coaster is a psychological thrill ride that will bring you face to face with the fear of darkness, insects, speed, and heights.

7 Transformers™: The Ride 3-D

Get caught in an intergalactic war between the heroic Autobots and the evil Decepticons in this popular ride.

9 The Wizarding World of Harry Potter

Marvel at the remarkable detail in Hogsmeade village and Hogwarts Castle **(above)**. The 3-D ride, Harry Potter and the Forbidden Journey, and the Flight of the Hippogriff roller coaster will keep you happy.

10 Water World®

For the best stunts, catch this show where the polar ice caps have melted and all land lies beneath the sea. Memorable moments include a crash-landing seaplane and fireballs.

📟🏅 Griffith Park

Griffith Park is a 6.7-sq-mile (17-sq-km) natural playground of rugged hills and gentle valleys, draped with native oak trees, manzanita, and sage. As well as hiking and horseback trails, there are picnic areas, golf courses, tennis courts, and an outdoor music venue. The country's largest urban park owes its existence to the Welshman Griffith Jenkins Griffith (1850–1919). In 1896, Griffith donated a large portion of his estate to the city with the proviso that it become "a place of recreation and rest for the masses."

② Los Angeles Zoo

Some 1,400 animals are found here *(see p59)*, including koalas and chimps. The breeding program has brought the California condor back from near-extinction.

① Autry Museum of the American West

This collection of art and artifacts **(above)** covers the history and mythology of the American West. Star exhibits include a Colt handgun collection.

③ Mount Hollywood Trail

The popular trek to the top of Mount Hollywood, the highest point in Griffith Park, rewards hikers with plenty of exercise and sweeping views of Los Angeles.

REBEL WITHOUT A CAUSE MEMORIAL

James Dean was one of Hollywood's big stars when, aged 24, he died in a car crash on a lone highway in Central California. A bronze bust outside the Griffith Park Observatory honors the actor, who filmed the famous knife-fight from *Rebel Without a Cause* on the steps of the building. The scene's intensity stems partly from the fact that the actors used real switchblades, though wearing protective vests. The bust is on the west side of the lawn.

④ Travel Town Museum

A fleet of vintage locomotives **(below)**, freight and passenger cars, and several cabooses (goods trains) draw railroad aficionados to this outdoor museum. Children love riding the miniature train.

⑤ Greek Theatre

A favorite LA outdoor concert venue, the 5,900-seat Greek Theatre *(see p64)* presents top musical talent in its leafy natural bowl setting from spring to fall.

6 Forest Lawn Memorial Park – Hollywood Hills

Buster Keaton and Bette Davis are among the celebrities interred in this parklike cemetery dotted with patriotic art and architecture.

7 Griffith Observatory and Planetarium

The observatory **(below)** has been the park's chief attraction since 1935. A renovation project added 40,000 sq ft (3,716 sq m) of public space.

Map of Griffith Park

8 Merry-Go-Round

A slice of nostalgia in the midst of futuristic LA, this beloved 1926 Spillman carousel has 68 exquisitely carved horses with real horse-hair tails.

9 Bronson Caves

Scenes from *Star Trek*, *Batman*, *Bonanza*, and countless other film and TV productions were shot in this former rock quarry and caves, tucked away in a remote corner of Griffith Park **(below)**.

NEED TO KNOW
MAP D1

Griffith Park: open 6am–10pm

Griffith Park Ranger Station: 4730 Crystal Springs Dr

Autry Museum of the American West: 4700 Western Heritage Way; open 10am–4pm Tue–Fri (to 5pm Sat & Sun); adm

Travel Town Museum: 5200 Zoo Dr; open 10am–5pm daily

Griffith Observatory: 2800 E Observatory Rd; 213-473-0800; open noon–10pm Tue–Fri (from 10am Sat & Sun)

Bronson Caves: Take Canyon Dr to the end, then take the path past the gate east of the last parking lot

Southern Railroad: open 10am–4:30pm Mon–Fri (to 5pm Sat & Sun)

■ The Café at the End of the Universe, inside the Observatory, serves hot and cold lunch options.

■ Sunset Ranch Hollywood (*3400 Beachwood Dr*) offers day and night horse rides through the park.

10 Griffith Park and Southern Railroad

Generations of children have boarded the three miniature trains that chug along a 1-mile (1.6-km) track past pony rides and a Wild West ghost town moving over a bridge, through a tunnel, past grazing goats and a picturesque cactus garden.

TOP 10 ★ Disneyland® Resort

Disneyland® Resort has been an iconic feature of Los Angeles since the theme park's inception in 1955. A second park, Disney California Adventure®, was added adjacent to the original in 2001. Downtown Disney®, a further addition, is an entertainment, restaurant, and retail district. The two parks, three Disney hotels, and Downtown Disney® together form Disneyland® Resort.

1 Meeting Mickey
Before meeting Mr. Mouse up close and personal, children are invited to stroll through his house and garden and visit one of his sets – Mickey's Toontown **(right)**.

2 Haunted Mansion
Dare to enter this mysterious mansion in New Orleans Square inhabited by 999 ghoulish spirits. Board a "Doom Buggy" for a chilling ride.

3 Matterhorn Bobsleds
The park's first roller coaster may look tame but it packs a punch. Strap into a bobsled for a bumpy but exhilarating ride. A must-do for kids.

4 Pirates of the Caribbean
Hold on to your hat as you plunge down into a watery world of darkness **(above)** where wicked pirates plunder the Caribbean.

5 Big Thunder Mountain Railroad
Hop on to this runaway mine train roller coaster in Frontierland for a journey through the Wild West. Charge through bat caverns and brave falling rocks.

6 Roger Rabbit's Car Toon Spin
Get ready for a wild ride in Mickey's Toontown as you pilot a runaway cab through the wacky world of Roger Rabbit.

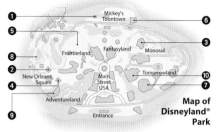

① ⑤ ⑧ ② ④ ⑨ ⑥ ③ ⑩ ⑦

Mickey's Toontown
Frontierland
Fantasyland
Monorail
New Orleans Square
Main Street U.S.A
Tomorrowland
Adventureland
Entrance

Map of Disneyland® Park

SHOWS, PARADES, AND PYROTECHNICS ③

Daily schedules vary but you may get to see Mickey's "Magic Happens" parade on Main Street, U.S.A with its explosive music and decorated floats. The skies are ablaze for a nightly fireworks extravaganza with popular songs from Disney movies. A seasonal highlight is Fantasmic!, a 25-minute live action evening special-effects show starring Mickey Mouse and other characters. Special shows are also set for the Christmas holidays, Lunar New Year, and Halloween.

⑦ Space Mountain

Soar by comets, stars, and solar systems while plunging into the unknown. Dips and sharp-banked turns will keep you clutching the edge of your rocket ship.

⑧ Tiana's Bayou Adventure

In late 2024, the Splash Mountain ride is expected to reopen as Tiana's Bayou Adventure, inspired by the only Black Disney princess in the animated film, *The Princess and the Frog* (2009).

⑨ Indiana Jones Adventure™

Join Indy on this bumpy ride through an old temple in Adventureland on a rickety jeep.

Star Tours: The Adventures Continue ⑩

This update of one of the park's iconic attractions in Tomorrowland (right) features a journey to the Planet Batuu and a visit to the Black Spire Outpost in 3-D.

NEED TO KNOW

MAP F4 ■ 1313 Harbor Blvd, Anaheim, about 30 miles (48 km) south of LA ■ 714-781-4565 ■ www.disney land.com

Disneyland®: open 8am–midnight daily; adm $104–$169; under 3s free

Disney California Adventure: open 8am–midnight daily; adm $109–$118

Off-peak Disneyland®: open 9am–6pm Mon–Fri, 9am–8pm Sat & Sun

■ Reservations are required at all times; check online for latest hours.

■ Dine at Wine Country Trattoria in Disney California Adventure® or at Blue Bayou in Disneyland®.

■ A ParkHopper ticket gives access to Disneyland and Disney California Adventure parks. Disneyland also offers two to five day passes.

Disneyland® Resort: California Adventure®

1 Pixar Pier

A popular addition to the park's beachy wonderland, this section features the thrilling Incredicoaster. Play games and win prizes at the interactive Toy Story Midway Mania! Other attractions include Pixar-themed food, the Lamplight Lounge, and more.

2 Pixar Pal-A-Round

You can't miss this enormous, 150-ft- (46-m-) tall Ferris wheel with a grinning Mickey Mouse on the front of it. Two different ride experiences are on offer: the red gondolas on the outer portion of the wheel are fixed – like any normal Ferris wheel – while the other gondolas on the inner part of the wheel swing around freely as they rotate around the wheel. Both feature your favorite Pixar characters and give stunning views of Paradise Bay.

3 Animation Academy

For about 15 minutes, a Disney animator gives you step-by-step instructions on drawing your favorite character, such as Mickey, Donald, or Goofy. Materials are supplied. You'll learn a few basic techniques, and you can take home your finished product.

4 Avengers Campus

This "land" lets you hop on board the Spider-Man Adventure for a fast-paced ride; encounter Dr. Strange among the ruins of Ancient Sanctum; or team up with Marvel heroes such as Black Widow, Iron Man, and The Wasp in the Quinjet building, which acts as the Avengers Headquarters. A plaque by the entrance honors Marvel Comics legend Stan Lee.

5 Grizzly River Run

Billed as the "world's highest, longest, and fastest," this thrilling

The thrilling Grizzly River Run

Radiator Springs Racers speeding through Ornament Valley

whitewater raft ride takes you on a churning trip through the Sierra Nevada foothills beneath a Grizzly bear-shaped mountaintop. Prepare to get drenched on this one.

6 Toy Story Midway Mania!

Put on your 3-D glasses and be transported to a world of classic American carnival-style games. Shoot darts at balloons, rings at aliens, eggs at barnyard targets, and more. Keep your wits about you and watch out for the special effects.

7 World of Color

A dramatic, whimsical, and dazzling water fountain show, World of Color is spectacular fun for the whole family. Special effects are played out on huge projection screens made from sprayed water, as images from Disney movies and characters run by. Brilliant colors burst, flame-throwers cast waves of flames 50 ft (15 m) into the air, and a musical score fills you with wonder.

8 Guardians of the Galaxy – Mission: BREAKOUT!

Experience the terrifying sensation of free falling in the dark surrounded by audio and visual effects. You'll join the Marvel Comics character, Rocket Raccoon, as he attempts to free other Guardians of the Galaxy figures who are imprisoned in glass display cases suspended over a bottomless pit. Drop sequences with a 'free fall' sensation are part of the fun.

9 Radiator Springs Racers

A smiling six-person convertible takes you on a scenic drive through Ornament Valley before your final preparation for the big race. Once lined up with another car full of guests, the green flag will drop and you'll begin a high-speed, flat-out race through the desert, past camelback hills, red rock formations, geysers, and banked turns.

The Soarin' Around the World ride

10 Soarin' Around the World

Lift off as you "fly" above CGI recreations of some famous landmarks – from the Golden Gate Bridge to the Great Wall of China – in this virtual hang-gliding adventure. This is the most memorable ride at Disney California Adventure®.

Disneyland® Resort: Practical Tips

E-Ticket Pool at Disneyland® Hotel

1 When to Visit
The parks are busiest during the summer, around Easter and Thanksgiving, and again between Christmas and New Year. Crowds thin out from January to March and November to mid-December.

2 Beating the Crowds
If you're visiting during peak periods, try to visit midweek instead of weekends and aim to arrive at least half an hour before the gates open, then head for your favorite rides first. Lines are usually shorter at lunchtime and during the parades.

3 Single Lines
If you don't mind riding alone or with a stranger, several attractions in both parks have "single lines" to fill any gaps. Usually these lines are much shorter.

Anna & Elsa's Boutique

4 Kids' Matters
Each park has baby care centers, boutiques and baby stroller rental stations. Some rides have minimum height requirements.

5 Get the App
The official Disneyland app offers custom itineraries and personalized park recommendations. It lets you book restaurants, hotels, and tickets, plus locate sights using GPS maps.

6 Souvenirs
Try not to stock up too early to avoid carrying souvenirs around all day. World of Disney at Downtown Disney® has the best selection.

7 Disney Hotels
Staying at one of the three official Disney hotels is not cheap, but they are convenient for access. Disney's Grand Californian *(see p149)* even has a direct entrance to Disney California Adventure Park®.

Hearthstone Lounge at a Disney Hotel

8 What to Bring and What to Wear
Wear comfortable shoes and clothes and bring a hat, sunscreen, and a sweater for the evening, even during the summer. It's all available in the park, but at inflated prices.

9 Hidden Mickeys
These can be found hidden throughout the park. People make a game of spotting them.

10 Lightning Lane
This $25 package, available in the Disneyland app, shows forecasted wait times. Plan your day and purchase arrival windows to skip long queues. High-demand attractions are limited.

WALT DISNEY'S VISION

Mad Tea Party at Disneyland Park

Walt Disney (1901–66), creator of Mickey Mouse, was a pioneer in the field of animation. A relentlessly driven and inventive man, he wished to share his brilliant imagination with families in a non-cinematic way. Watching his own children at play in an ordinary amusement park, Disney was inspired to build a place that was clean and filled with attractions for both parents and kids. Walt Disney envisioned a theme park with five lands: Main Street, a setting plucked from late 19th- and early 20th-century America; Adventureland; Frontierland, paying homage to the Wild West; futuristic Tomorrowland; and Fantasyland, inspired by the song *When You Wish Upon a Star*. Disney picked a 160-acre (65-ha) site in Anaheim and oversaw every aspect of the planning and construction of Disneyland®. When the Magic Kingdom opened its gates in 1955, and 28,000 people stormed in, tears reportedly streamed down Walt Disney's cheeks – his great dream had finally become a reality.

TOP 10 DISNEY BY NUMBERS

1 Over 750 million guests since opening

2 1 million annuals planted at Disneyland every year

3 Eight US presidents have visited

4 1.2 million gallons of soft drinks sold annually

5 5,000 gallons of paint used each year

6 300 species of plants grow throughout the resort

7 34,000 employees ("cast members")

8 4 million hamburgers consumed annually

9 30 tons of trash collected every day

10 100,000 light bulbs illuminate the resort

Walt Disney unveils his plans for Disneyland to a national television audience during the premiere of the television show "Disneyland".

TOP 10 ⭐ Catalina Island

This island may be only 22 miles (35 km) across the sea, but it's a world away from the urban velocity of LA. Ferries dock in Avalon, the island's commercial hub. Most of the interior is a protected nature preserve that may only be explored on foot or bicycle (permit required), or by organized tour. These are excellent ways to learn about the island's history as a destination for sea otter poachers, smugglers, Union soldiers, and mining speculators.

1 Green Pleasure Pier

This green pier has been the hub of Avalon activity since 1909. For years, it was the official weighing station for game-fishing enthusiasts.

2 Lover's Cove

Rent a snorkel and take to the clear blue waters of this poetically named marine preserve teeming with golden Garibaldi (California's state marine fish).

3 Wrigley Memorial and Botanic Gardens

The monument to William Wrigley Jr., of Wrigley's chewing gum, built in 1935, towers over vast gardens (**below**). Plants include species unique to the island.

4 Avalon Casino

This Art Deco landmark, built for William Wrigley Jr., opened in 1929 and was never a gambling place. It contains a movie theater and a ballroom that once hosted nationally broadcast concerts. Murals of underwater scenes adorn the exterior.

A WEALTH OF WILDLIFE

Catalina has a unique ecosystem and includes such endemic species as the Channel Island fox and the Catalina ground squirrel. The introduction of non-native animals resulted in overgrazing, a trend the Catalina Island Conservancy is now seeking to reverse. Another restoration project has returned the California bald eagle to the skies. Pelicans, gulls, and cormorants can also be spotted. The ocean waters are abundant with sea lions, Garibaldi, flying fish, and shark.

Map of Catalina Island

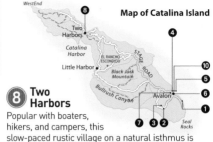

WestEnd

Two Harbors

Catalina Harbor

EL RANCHO ESCONDIDO

Little Harbor

Black Jack Mountain

STAGE ROAD

Bullrush Canyon

Avalon

Seal Rocks

⑤ Casino Point Dive Park

This reserve, set up in 1965, was California's first city-designated water park and is great for divers **(above)**.

⑧ Two Harbors

Popular with boaters, hikers, and campers, this slow-paced rustic village on a natural isthmus is about 23 miles (37 km) west of Avalon. It is served by ferry from the mainland and by bus from Avalon.

Green Pleasure Pier and Avalon Casino

⑥ Nature Center at Avalon Canyon

Here, hands-on activities and exhibits showcase the biodiversity of the Island.

⑦ Catalina Country Club

In 1929, Wrigley Jr. made this the spring training ground of his baseball team. The clubhouse is now a restaurant.

⑨ Catalina Buffalo

Island explorations may lead to encounters with herds of chocolate-colored buffalo **(right)**. The first 14 animals were brought here in 1924 for a Zane Grey film.

⑩ Catalina Island Museum

Over 7,000 years of island history come alive here, with artifacts, pottery, and photographs from Catalina's days as the darling of Hollywood.

NEED TO KNOW

Visitors' Bureau: Green Pleasure Pier; 310-510-1520

Wrigley Memorial and Botanic Gardens: www. catalinaconservancy. org; adm

Nature Center at Avalon Canyon: www.catalina conservancy.org

Catalina Island Museum: www.catalina museum.org; adm

Catalina Express: 800-481-3470; www.catalina express.com

Catalina Island Company: 877-778-8322

Catalina Adventure Tours: 844-230-3821

▪ Try the Lobster Trap for fresh fish and Steve's Steakhouse for meat.

▪ Go swimming, kayaking, snorkeling, or take a glass-bottom boat tour.

▪ Catalina is at its best in the evening, after the last ferry has whisked off most of the tourists, so consider an overnight stay.

The Top 10
of Everything

A lifeguard tower on Venice Beach

🔟 Moments in History

1 Pre-1780s: Early Settlers

For at least 5,000 years before the first Europeans arrived, the LA basin was home to about 100 villages inhabited by Indigenous people collectively known as the Tongva. Gabrieleño-Tongva and other prominent Indigenous groups still live in and around modern-day Los Angeles.

2 1781: The Founding of Los Angeles

Under orders of King Carlos III of Spain, the governor of California Felipe de Neve laid out a small settlement along a river valley and, on September 4, called it El Pueblo de la Reina de Los Angeles (the Town of the Queen of the Angels) *(see p77)*.

3 1850: LA Becomes a City

After the US-Mexican War (1846–48), Los Angeles became part of the US on April 4, five months before California became the 31st state. With a population of only 1,600, it lacked even such basic urban infrastructures as graded roads and street lights.

4 1911: The Movies Come to LA

British immigrants David and William Horsely founded Hollywood's first permanent movie studio, the Nestor Film Company, in an old tavern at the corner of Sunset Boulevard and Gower Street, a site now occupied by a production studio. Within a decade, the district became the world's movie capital, and, by the 1930s and 1940s, Hollywood had officially entered its "Golden Age."

The LA aqueduct in the desert

5 1913: The Opening of the LA Aqueduct

"There it is! Take it!" is how William Mulholland, father of the world's longest aqueduct, famously greeted the first spurt of water to arrive in LA from the Owens Valley, some 250 miles (400 km) north, on November 5. Even today, the LA aqueduct continues to supply over 75 percent of the water needed by the residents of this metropolis, which is partly located in a subtropical desert.

6 The 1920s: The Birth of the Aviation Industry

In possession of just $1,000, but driven by a dream, 28-year-old Donald Douglas began designing airplanes in the back of a barber shop. A year later, the first Cloudster cargo plane propelled his

Donald Douglas and his partner David Davis

Douglas Aircraft Company into prominence. It went on to become one of the world's leading commercial airplane manufacturers.

7 1970: The Chicano Moratorium

The peaceful protest against the Vietnam War attracted more than 20,000 demonstrators. But clashes with the LAPD resulted in hundreds of arrests and three deaths.

8 1992: The LA Riots

Violence erupted again on April 29 after the acquittal of four white police officers on trial for beating up Black motorist Rodney King – an incident captured on videotape. The six days of rioting resulted in 55 dead and 2,300 injured.

9 1994: Northridge Earthquake

Millions were jolted awake on January 17 by a violent earthquake measuring 6.7 on the Richter scale. It caused 57 deaths and 6,500 injuries, interrupting water, electrical, and gas services, and damaging freeways and homes.

Northridge earthquake damage

10 2023: SAG-AFTRA and WGA Strike

In 2023, the American actors' union SAG-AFTRA and the Writers Guild of America (WGA) went on strike over an ongoing labor dispute with the Alliance of Motion Picture and Television Producers (AMPTP). This is the longest and most costly labor strike in Hollywood history and has impacted most film and TV production.

TOP 10 LA KEY FIGURES

Charlotta Spears Bass

1 Felipe de Neve (1728–84)
The Spanish governor who founded Los Angeles in 1781.

2 Phineas Banning (1830–85)
The "Father of Los Angeles Harbor," who also constructed Southern California's first railroad in 1869.

3 William Mulholland (1855–1935)
The chief engineer of Los Angeles's Water Department.

4 George Freeth (1883–1916)
This Hawaiian-Irish athlete introduced surfing to Southern California in the early 1900s.

5 Harrison Gray Otis (1837–1917)
City booster and publisher of the *Los Angeles Times* for three decades.

6 Charlotta Spears Bass (1874–1969)
Owner of the African American newspaper *The California Eagle* and the first Black woman to run for vice president of the United States in 1952.

7 Rubén Salazar (1928–1970)
Los Angeles Times' first Latino columnist who was shot by the LAPD during the Chicano Moratorium in 1970.

8 Dorothy Chandler (1901–1997)
Organizer of fundraisers that saved the Hollywood Bowl and created the Los Angeles Music Center.

9 Tom Bradley (1917–98)
LA's first African American mayor governed for an unprecedented five terms – from 1973 to 1993.

10 Karen Bass (1953–)
The first female mayor of LA, who has served as the 43rd mayor since 2022.

🔟 Architectural Landmarks

3 Schindler House

MAP M4 ■ 835 N Kings Rd, West Hollywood ■ Open 11am–6pm Wed–Sun ■ Adm

The once-private home and studio of Vienna-born architect Rudolf Schindler (1887–1953) is a modern architectural classic. Completed in 1922, the house has a flat roof, open floor plan, ample use of glass, and rooms opening to a courtyard. It greatly influenced California architecture and today, it houses the MAK Center for Art and Architecture, which hosts a year-round schedule of architectural tours, exhibitions, lectures, and other interesting events.

1 The Getty Center

The architecture of the extraordinary Getty Center (see pp16–19) is said to outshine the art displayed within its galleries. Architect Richard Meier created an elegant, sophisticated space that is nevertheless warmly welcoming.

2 Walt Disney Concert Hall

This Frank Gehry-designed (see p64) Downtown extravaganza is easily recognized by its shiny and dynamically curved exterior. Home of the Los Angeles Philharmonic Orchestra (see p78), it seats over 2,000 people. The city-block-sized complex also contains two outdoor amphitheaters.

4 Theme Building at Los Angeles International Airport

MAP H2 ■ 201 World Way ■ Closed to the public

Since 1961, a flying saucer has made its home in the center of LAX. The architectural firm of Pereira and Luckman found inspiration for their design in Southern California's unique Googie style of futurist architecture, inspired by space, cars and jets. In 2018, it became home for Bob Hope's USO for military members.

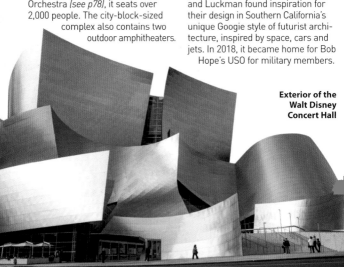

Exterior of the Walt Disney Concert Hall

Bradbury Building atrium

5 Bradbury Building
MAP V5 ■ 304 S Broadway
■ Closed to the public

This light-flooded 1893 office building, with its open-cage elevators, frilly iron work, and marble floors, is one of LA's top architectural landmarks. Architect George Wyman allegedly accepted the job after consulting a Ouija board. Movie buffs might recognize it from *Blade Runner* and *Chinatown*.

6 Chiat/Day Building
MAP B5 ■ 340 Main St, Venice
■ Closed to the public

Reflecting architect Frank Gehry's sculptural approach, this building was commissioned by advertising firm Chiat/Day as its West Coast corporate headquarters in 1991. Today, it's the home of Google's Venice campus and at its center is a three-story-tall pair of binoculars by Claes Oldenburg and Coosje van Bruggen, while the rust-colored columns on the right resemble a deconstructed forest.

7 The Gamble House
This stunning Pasadena Craftsman bungalow *(see p95)* marks the pinnacle of the career of Charles and Henry Greene. Built in 1908 as the retirement home of David and Mary Gamble of the Procter & Gamble family, the house has a beautiful garden, wide terraces, and open sleeping porches.

8 The Malin House
MAP D2 ■ 776 Torreyson Dr, Hollywood Hills ■ Closed to the public

John Lautner's bold, often experimental architectural style is exemplified in this private home in the Hollywood Hills. Resembling a flying saucer on a concrete column, it was built in 1960, the same year President John F. Kennedy launched the challenge to put a man on the moon. The house was featured in Brian de Palma's 1984 movie *Body Double*.

9 Hollyhock House
One of Frank Lloyd Wright's masterpieces of avant-garde architecture, the 1921 Hollyhock House *(see p101)* was the architect's first LA commission. Anchoring Barnsdall Art Park, the house takes full advantage of the mild California climate. Wright created seamless transitions between indoor and outdoor space and made use of patios, porches, and rooftop terraces.

Hollyhock House

10 Cathedral of Our Lady of the Angels
Behind the fortress-like exterior of the cathedral *(see p78)*, designed by José Rafael Moneo, awaits a minimalist hall of worship, where the lack of right angles and supporting pillars creates a sense of spacious loftiness. You don't have to be a Roman Catholic to appreciate the lovely tapestries of the nave, depicting dozens of saints.

🔟 Beaches

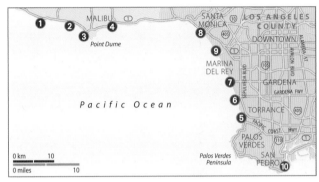

1 Nicholas Canyon Beach
33900 block of Pacific Coast Hwy, near Ventura County Line

This lovely 2-mile (3-km) beach is quieter than most in Malibu because of its isolation and distance from the city. It hugs the base of a bluff and is a great place for those seeking solitude and a tan.

Rock formations at El Matador Beach

2 El Matador Beach
32350 block of Pacific Coast Hwy, Malibu

Rugged, secluded, and dotted with large boulders eroded by nature, this small cliff-backed beach is one of LA's finest. Its remoteness, limited parking, and cumbersome access via an uneven trail keep the crowds at bay. There are limited facilities, but you can explore tide pools and caves. Nude sunbathing is illegal in LA County but some does occur.

3 Zuma Beach
30000 block of Pacific Coast Hwy, Malibu

This 2-mile (3-km) ribbon of fine, sparkling sand is one of LA's most popular beaches. Its clean water and mid-sized waves are great for bodysurfing and swimming. It teems with families on summer Sundays but is nearly deserted the rest of the week, making it perfect for quiet picnics and walks along the beach.

4 Malibu Lagoon State/ Surfrider Beach
MAP A2 ▪ 23050 block of Pacific Coast Hwy, Malibu

Wedged in between the Malibu Pier and the gated celebrity enclave, Malibu Colony, this popular beach (see p121) offers many diversions. Watch surfers shred the waves at Surfrider Beach. The eponymous lagoon is a stopover for migratory birds, while the nearby Adamson House with its idyllic gardens overlooks Malibu Pier and Malibu Lagoon.

5 Redondo Beach
MAP D4

A unique horseshoe-shaped pier lined with shops, arcades, and food stands is Redondo Beach's focal point. Rent a paddleboard or kayak and hit the water, or take a bicycle along the cycle path. Boutiques and art galleries are just a few blocks inland.

6 Hermosa Beach
MAP C3 ■ Around Pier Ave

South of Manhattan Beach, Hermosa *(see p123)* has a busy bar and restaurant scene right where Pier Avenue meets the sand. Beach volleyball is the local pastime and national tournaments take place throughout the year. Only the paved South Bay Bicycle Trail that runs from Marina del Rey to Palos Verdes lies between the sand and private homes.

7 Manhattan Beach
MAP C3 ■ Manhattan Beach Blvd

The Beach Boys, who grew up near here and Hermosa Beach, found inspiration for their inimitable surf music in the white sands and glorious waves of this upscale yet relaxed seaside town. Longboarders still compete for the perfect ride, especially around the Manhattan Pier, which is home to the Roundhouse Marine Studies Lab and Aquarium.

8 Santa Monica Beach
MAP A4 ■ Along Pacific Coast Hwy in Santa Monica

This easy-to-access beach *(see p59)* is one of LA's busiest. Families love the Santa Monica Pier *(see p121)* with its pretty carousel and amusement park. Fitness buffs can get their kicks from pedaling or skating down a paved path running past the original Muscle Beach, the birthplace of the Southern California exercise craze back in the 1930s.

Ocean Front Walk, Venice Beach

9 Venice Beach
MAP A5 ■ Ocean Front Walk between Venice Blvd & Rose Ave

Founded in 1925 as a seaside resort town, Venice Beach *(see p122)* soon merged with LA to become one of the city's most diverse neighborhoods. Beach supplies can be bought here and there are plenty of outdoor areas for activities. The beach makes for a prime people-watching spot.

10 Cabrillo Beach
MAP D5 ■ Stephen M. White Dr, San Pedro

The sails of windsurfers flutter like giant butterflies along this beach on the breakwater of LA Harbor. Visit the nearby Cabrillo Marine Aquarium to learn about marine life.

Santa Monica Pier

🔟 Parks and Gardens

① Huntington Library, Art Museum, and Botanical Gardens

A perfect synthesis of nature and culture, this amazing estate *(see pp28–31)* houses priceless collections of paintings and rare manuscripts that were started by railroad tycoon Henry E. Huntington and his wife Arabella in the early 19th century.

Fountain at Greystone Mansion

② Greystone Mansion and Park

MAP J3 ▪ 905 Loma Vista Dr, Beverly Hills ▪ 310-285-6830 ▪ Open 10am–6pm daily; call for park hours; mansion open for special events only ▪ www.greystonemansion.org

Popular with wedding planners and visitors in search of solitude, this secluded park affords great views of Beverly Hills. Its centerpiece is a 55-room mansion built in 1928 by oil tycoon Edward Doheny as a wedding present for his son Ned. The estate has been featured in many movies, including *Air Force One*.

③ Griffith Park

The country's largest urban park *(see pp34–5)* is filled with museums, entertainment for children, hiking and horse trails, and the famous Griffith Observatory.

④ Virginia Robinson Gardens

MAP J4 ▪ 1008 Elden Way ▪ 310-550-2087 ▪ Tours: 10am–1pm on select days; call for schedule ▪ Adm ▪ www.robinsongardens.org

The 1911 estate of department-store heiress Virginia Robinson is one of the oldest in Beverly Hills. Stroll in gardens with fountains and statuettes past towering king palms and elegant camellias flourishing in this quiet hideaway.

⑤ Exposition Park Rose Garden

MAP D2 ▪ 701 State Dr ▪ 9am–sunset daily (closed Jan 1–Mar 15) ▪ www.laparks.org/exporosegarden/rosegarden.htm

This lovely rose garden dates back to 1928 and features about 15,000 rose bushes that bloom from March through November. Great for picnics or for a respite from museums.

⑥ Wrigley Mansion and Gardens

The winter home of William Wrigley Jr. (of Wrigley's chewing gum) *(see p92)* is backed by a lovely green rose garden and now serves as the headquarters of the Pasadena Tournament of Roses Association.

Meditation at the Self-Realization Fellowship Lake Shrine

7 Self-Realization Fellowship Lake Shrine

MAP C2 ▪ 17190 Sunset Blvd
▪ 310-454-4114 ▪ 10am–4:30pm
Wed–Sun; reservation required
▪ www.lakeshrine.org

Bathed in an ambience of beauty and serenity, this hidden sanctuary was created in 1950 by Paramahansa Yogananda, an Indian-born spiritual leader. Wander over to the shrine to Mahatma Gandhi or the spring-fed lake, meditate inside a re-created 16th-century windmill, or study the Court of Religions that honors all of the world's major faiths.

8 Franklin D. Murphy Sculpture Garden

MAP C2 ▪ UCLA campus, Westwood
▪ Open daily ▪ www.hammer.ucla.edu

Tucked away in the northeastern corner of the UCLA campus, this delightful little oasis is dotted with 70 sculptures by some of the greatest 19th- and 20th-century European and American artists such as Auguste Rodin and Alexander Calder.

9 Runyon Canyon Park

MAP N1 ▪ At the end of Fuller St off Franklin Ave ▪ 323-666-5046
▪ Open until sunset (avoid after dark)

Minutes from the Walk of Fame, this area with moderately difficult trails has a colorful history – the ruins near the Fuller Steet entrance were built in 1930 by opera star John McCormack, and Errol Flynn lived in one of the pool houses in the late 1950s.

10 Palisades Park

MAP A3 ▪ Ocean Ave between Santa Monica Pier & San Vincente Blvd ▪ Open daily

Famous for its swaying palm trees and picture-perfect views of Santa Monica Bay (especially at sunset), Palisades Park is a playground for young and old, locals and visitors, families and courting couples. Stretching for 13 blocks atop a bluff overlooking the ocean, the park has benches and lawns that invite picnics and people-watching. A nostalgic curiosity is the Camera Obscura inside the seniors' center at 1450 Ocean Avenue.

Palisades Park

🔟 Off the Beaten Path

① Echo Park Time Travel Mart

MAP D2 ▪ 1714 Sunset Blvd, Echo Park ▪ Open noon–6pm daily ▪ www.timetravelmart.com

This niche store sells a range of quirky time travel-themed goods, including dinosaur eggs, robot milk, and retro alarm clocks. It was created by the nonprofit organization 826LA, which assists young Angeleno writers through tutoring sessions and creative workshops. All proceeds from the store go towards supporting the students, whose published works are also available for purchase instore.

② Museum of Latin American Art

MAP E4 ▪ 628 Alamitos Ave, Long Beach ▪ 562-437-1689 ▪ Open 11am–6pm Wed–Sun ▪ Adm (free for under 12s) ▪ www.molaa.org

Part of Long Beach's emerging creative arts scene, this museum is the only one in the United States dedicated to showcasing the modern and contemporary works of Latin American artists. A permanent collection of 1,500 works, traveling exhibitions, and a sculpture garden instruct and inspire.

Museum of Latin American Art

Book tunnel at The Last Bookstore

③ The Last Bookstore

MAP V5 ▪ 453 Spring St ▪ 213-488-0599 ▪ Open 11am–8pm daily ▪ www.lastbookstorela.com

An abandoned bank has transformed into a world devoted to the love of reading and books as art. It's not just another bookstore, but a Downtown destination where devotees come to explore 250,000 titles, pass through a book tunnel, or wander the adjacent art galleries.

④ Watts Towers

MAP E3 ▪ 1765 E 107th St, Watts ▪ 213-847-4646 ▪ www.wattstowers.org

This folk-art masterpiece is a whimsical trio of spires, adorned with rainbow-colored pieces of tile, glass, pottery, shells, and other scavenged materials. The sculpture, completed in 1954, represents the life's work of Italian immigrant Simon Rodia. Adjacent is their arts center, which hosts free educational classes.

⑤ Metro Art

www.art.metro.net

Stations throughout the Metro Rail system exhibit delightful murals, sculpture, artwork, and photography reflective of the local neighborhood around the stop. These award-winning installations represent the work of more than 100 different artists. Be sure to download art guides for the different rail lines you plan to use in advance.

Previous pages Stunning aerial view of Venice Beach

6 Los Angeles Maritime Museum

MAP D4 ■ Berth 84, at the foot of 6th St, San Pedro ■ Open noon–5pm Wed–Sun ■ Adm ■ www.lamaritimemuseum.org

This museum celebrates LA's seafaring tradition through displays of nautical models and memorabilia. A highlight is the exhibit about the USS *Los Angeles*, a navy cruiser that fought in China and the Korean War. Nearby is the Battleship USS *Iowa* Museum. The highlight here is the USS *Iowa*, which transported Roosevelt across the Atlantic to meet Churchill during World War II.

7 Museum of Jurassic Technology

9341 Venice Blvd, Culver City ■ 310-836-6131 ■ Opening hours vary, check website ■ Adm (free for under 12s) ■ www.mjt.org

The doors of this bizarre yet fun museum open up a parallel universe, where the seemingly mundane becomes extraordinary. A throwback to the natural science museums of the 19th century, exhibits include Cameroonian stink ants and a display of stereo floral radiography.

8 Paramount Ranch

2903 Cornell Rd, Agoura Hills ■ nps.gov

The mountains surrounding LA have provided a natural backdrop for Westerns since the 1920s, and the old buildings of Paramount Ranch have featured in many of the productions. Aside from an occasional film shoot, the ranch is open to explore, as are the adjacent hiking trails of the scenic Santa Monica Mountains National Recreation Area.

9 Sierra Madre

MAP F1

Just east of Pasadena, Sierra Madre is the type of old-fashioned town you can't imagine existing in the LA urban landscape. It is home to many of LA's creative artists, and a delightful mix of boutiques and cafés line the town center. Residential streets hold a number of original Craftsman houses. Visit in March for the annual Wistaria Festival.

10 Vasquez Rocks

10700 Escondido Canyon Rd, Agua Dulce ■ 661-268-0840 ■ www.parks.lacounty.gov

On the National Register of Historic places for its significance as a pre-historic site for the Shosone and Tataviam peoples, this 1.5-sq-mile (3.8-sq-km) natural desert park with its rock formations has found fame as a film location site for movie, TV, and music video productions from *Star Trek* to *The Flintstones*. Wear hiking boots and bring along a picnic.

The majestic Vasquez Rocks

🔟 Children's Attractions

1 California Science Center

Located in Exposition Park, this interactive museum *(see p86)* makes science and technology fun. Feel a simulated earthquake, explore LA's ecosystems, and marvel at the inner workings of a 50-ft (15-m) long robot named Tess. The adjoining Air and Space Gallery focuses on the principles of flight and space exploration.

Tess at the California Science Center

2 Universal Studios Hollywood^SM

This theme park *(see pp32–3)* attached to the world's largest movie studio is LA's biggest tourist attraction. A ticket buys a day of thrill rides and live action shows, and includes encounters with Harry Potter, King Kong, and other movie icons. A must-do is the narrated tram tour to the famous backlot sets.

3 Natural History Museum

This engaging museum *(see p85)* pays homage to the entire animal kingdom, including extinct species such as the perennially popular dinosaurs. Special child-oriented facilities include the Discovery Center, stocked with puppets, storybooks, and a fossil-rubbing station, and the Insect Zoo, home to a host of creepy crawlies.

4 Cabrillo Marine Aquarium

MAP D5 ▪ 3720 Stephen White Dr, San Pedro ▪ 310-548-7562 ▪ Open noon–5pm Tue–Fri, 10am–5pm Sat & Sun ▪ Donation ▪ www.cabrillomarine-aquarium.org

This facility offers an entertaining introduction to life in Southern California's ocean waters. The playful yet educational exhibits are ideal for children. Activities include guided tide pool walks, a marine laboratory workshop, and Marine Biology Summer Day Camps for kids.

5 Aquarium of the Pacific

MAP E4 ▪ 100 Aquarium Way, Long Beach ▪ 562-590-3100 ▪ Open 9am–6pm daily ▪ Adm ▪ www.aquariumofpacific.org

Take a virtual dive through three regions of the Pacific Ocean at this aquarium. Explore the kelp beds of Southern California, the stormy shores of the north Pacific, and the coral reefs of the tropical Pacific. "Dive charts" help you identify the species.

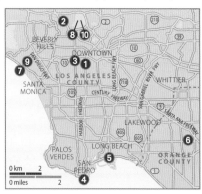

The popular Pacific Park® at the Santa Monica Pier

6 Santa Monica Pier

Visitors can take to the skies in a Ferris wheel, or watch local fisherfolk reel in their latest catch at this pier. These are just some of the activities on California's oldest operating amusement pier (see p121), where attractions draw over four million people a year. During summer, a free concert series takes place on Thursday nights.

7 Disneyland®

Nearly 70 years after it first opened its doors, the "magic kingdom" (see pp36–41) continues to be right on top of most children's must-see lists. A one-, two-, or three-day visit is guaranteed to delight, amaze, and exhaust the kids, especially since the entire resort also includes a second theme park, Disney's California Adventure®, and the Downtown Disney® entertainment district to Disneyland®.

8 Griffith Park

LA's largest municipal park, Griffith Park (see pp34–5) has plenty of activities for families and children. Hop on a merry-go-round from 1926, ride on a miniature railway at the Travel Town Museum or learn about stars and space at the Griffith Observatory with its telescopes, museum, and fantastic planetarium.

9 Cayton Children's Museum

MAP K6 ■ Suite 374, 395 Santa Monica Place ■ Open 10am–5pm Wed–Sun ■ Adm ■ www.cayton-museum.org

Located in the Santa Monica Place mall, this fun venue features free-form objects, round rooms, and an open air plan. Hands-on exhibits include the Courage Climber rope canopy and the Hello Booth with phones powered by imagination.

10 Los Angeles Zoo

MAP D1 ■ 5333 Zoo Dr ■ Open 10am–5pm daily ■ Closed 25 Dec ■ Adm (free for under 2s) ■ www.lazoo.org

The Campo Gorilla Reserve and the Winnick Family Children's Zoo, both are favorites at the LA Zoo. See barnyard animals at Muriel's Ranch, greet the baby animals in the nursery, and ride on the Safari Shuttle, hopping on and off at six stops around the zoo.

Queues outside Los Angeles Zoo

Hollywood Connections

Costumes of the Suicide Squad characters at the Warner Bros. Studio Tour

1 Warner Bros. Studio Tour
MAP D1 ■ 3400 Warner Blvd, Burbank ■ 818-977-8687 ■ Adm ■ www.wbstudiotour.com

A three-hour tour offering a thorough look at both the history as well as the day-to-day working reality of a major motion picture studio. Watch an introductory movie, visit the outdoor sets, and museum. Tour routes vary.

2 Sony Pictures Studio Tour
MAP D2 ■ 10202 W Washington Blvd, Culver City ■ 310-244-8687 ■ Tours: Mon–Fri, call for schedule, reservations required ■ Adm

This giant movie lot was the historic home of the famous MGM, producer of well-known classics such as *The Wizard of Oz*, until purchased by Sony in 1990. The two-hour walking tour may include a visit to the set of the game show *Jeopardy*.

A set at the Sony Pictures Studio

3 Larry Edmunds Bookshop
MAP P2 ■ 6644 Hollywood Blvd ■ 323-463-3273 ■ www.larry edmunds.com

Books about animation, acting, and Hollywood history, as well as historic movie posters, publicity stills, and screenplays – this store has it all.

4 American Cinematheque
To listen to Hollywood actors and directors discuss movies, attend screenings by this group *(see p62)* at the historic Egyptian Theatre *(see p13)*. The schedule ranges from retrospectives to filmmaker tributes.

5 It's a Wrap!
MAP D1 ■ 3315 W Magnolia Blvd, Burbank ■ 818-567-7366 ■ www.itsawraphollywood.com

Much of the clothing worn by actors ends up here. There are bargains galore, and each item sports a tag identifying the show it appeared in.

6 TMZ Celebrity Tour
MAP P2 ■ 6925 Hollywood Blvd ■ 855-486-9868 ■ Tours: check website for timings ■ Adm ■ www. tmztour.com

This two-hour, open-air bus tour is run by the TV show, *TMZ*. Guides are poised to spot celebrities and interview them on the street. An edgy, fast look at current hot star hangouts.

7 Hollywood Mega Store

MAP D2 ▪ 940 W Washington Blvd ▪ 213-747-9239 ▪ Open 9am–4pm Mon–Thu, 9am–2pm Fri ▪ www.hollywoodmegastore.com

This vast warehouse features thousands of movie-related items, including novelty gifts, original posters and photos, party items, and merchandise licensed by Disney, Warner Bros., and Universal Studios.

8 Paramount Pictures Studio Tour

MAP R4 ▪ 5515 Melrose Ave ▪ 323-956-1777 ▪ Adm ▪ www.paramountstudiotour.com

See the famous New York backlot and learn about the history of this working movie studio on a two-hour tour. Reservations are required.

Paramount Pictures Studio entrance

9 Margaret Herrick Library

MAP L6 ▪ 333 S La Cienega Blvd, Beverly Hills ▪ 310-247-3000 ▪ Open 10am–6pm Mon, Tue, Thu, & Fri ▪ ID required

It's easy to get lost in this repository of movie-related books and publications, operated by the Academy of Motion Picture Arts and Sciences.

10 The Real Hollywood Tour

www.thereallosangelestours.com

Learn about the origins of Hollywood as a small farming town in the early 20th century and discover how it became the center of the motion picture industry on this walking tour full of historic and iconic sights.

TOP 10 FILM LOCATIONS

The colorful Bradbury Building

1 Bradbury Building
You might recognize the striking architecture of this building from films such as *Blade Runner* (1982) and *500 Days of Summer* (2009).

2 Griffith Park Observatory
This timeless building famously appeared in *Rebel Without a Cause* (1955) and *La La Land* (2016).

3 Rodeo Drive
Julia Roberts went on a shopping spree along this luxury street in *Pretty Woman* (1990).

4 Chinatown
Filming location for Roman Polanski's Oscar-nominated *Chinatown* (1974).

5 Occidental College
Fans of the 1990s movie *Clueless* may recognize this campus as Cher's school. Much of the movie was also filmed in and around Beverly Hills.

6 Fox Plaza
This towering office block was the setting for the 1980s classic *Die Hard*.

7 Millennium Biltmore Hotel
Scenes from *Ghostbusters* (1984), *Pretty in Pink* (1986), and *Beverly Hills Cop* (1984) were filmed in this hotel.

8 Point Dume State Beach
The iconic ending of *Planet of the Apes* (1968) was filmed on this scenic beach.

9 Vasquez Rocks
Trekkies will be familiar with this park's dramatic landscape, which served as a backdrop in numerous *Star Trek* films.

10 Bob's Big Boy
This beloved LA diner appeared in the 1995 action movie *Heat*.

🔟 Movie Theaters

① AMC The Grove 14
MAP N5 ▪ 189 The Grove Dr, Midtown ▪ 323-879-6948

State-of-the-art meets Art Deco charm at this 14-screen complex that evokes the grand theaters of early LA. Great for star sightings.

AMC The Grove 14

② New Beverly Cinema
MAP P5 ▪ 7165 Beverly Blvd ▪ www.thenewbev.com

Owned by Quentin Tarantino, this single-screen theater shows movies only on celluloid film. Significant upgrades in 2018 have refreshed the space.

③ Cinemark Howard Hughes Los Angeles & XD
MAP D3 ▪ 6081 Center Dr, off Fwy 405 ▪ 310-568-3375

This cutting-edge theater has been aptly subtitled "cinema de lux". Enjoy recently released movies while sitting in large and luxurious leather chairs.

④ ArcLight Cinemas and Cinerama Dome
MAP Q3 ▪ 6360 W Sunset Blvd ▪ 323-464-4226 ▪ **Temporarily closed for renovations**

The exquisite 15-screen ArcLight is the shiny neighbor of the futuristic Cinerama Dome (see p101). The lobby leads to a lively café-bar with terrace. Good for star sightings.

⑤ The Egyptian Theatre
MAP P2 ▪ 6712 Hollywood Blvd ▪ 323-466-3456

This themed 1920s movie palace (see p13) was purchased by Netflix in 2020. American Cinematheque (see p60) has a long contract to screen movies on the weekends, with Netflix doing weekday shows.

⑥ California Science Center IMAX Theater
MAP D2 ▪ 700 Exposition Park Dr ▪ 323-744-7400 ▪ www.california sciencecenter.org

IMAX stands for "maximum image" and with a screen that is seven-stories tall and 90-ft (27-m) wide (see p86), it's a fitting name. A 12-channel surround-sound system ensures total sensory immersion.

California Science Center IMAX Theater

⑦ The Nuart Theatre
MAP C2 ■ 11272 Santa Monica Blvd ■ 310-473-8530 ■ www.landmarktheaters.com

One of LA's finest independent theaters, this shows movies that most multiplexes would avoid. The cult classic *The Rocky Horror Picture Show* still runs every Saturday.

⑧ TCL Chinese Theatre
MAP P2 ■ 6925 Hollywood Blvd ■ 323-461-3331

This flashy 1927 Chinese fantasy palace *(see p12)* is still the site of movie premieres. Catch a block-buster here – you may get to sit next to a celebrity. The sixplex next door has none of the original's historic flair.

TCL Chinese Theatre

⑨ The Academy Museum
MAP M6 ■ 6067 Wilshire Blvd ■ www.academymuseum.org

The gilded Academy Museum of Motion Pictures is the largest museum in the US dedicated to the history, art, and business of movie-making. Two state-of-the-art theaters screen archival works on most days.

⑩ El Capitan Theatre
MAP P2 ■ 6838 Hollywood Blvd ■ 323-467-7674

Old-time Hollywood glamour has returned to LA courtesy of the famed Walt Disney Company, which restored this 1926 theater in 1990 *(see p13)*. It now functions as a first-run cinema showing Disney flicks, sometimes preceded by lavish live shows.

TOP 10 OSCAR FACTS

Oscar statue inside Dolby Theatre

1 How the Oscar got its Name
The statuette got its name in 1931 after future Academy executive Margaret Herrick said it resembled her uncle Oscar.

2 Oscar by Numbers
The 13.5-inch (34-cm) tall, 8.5-lb (3.9-kg) Oscar has been handed to winners more than 3,100 times.

3 Top Four Oscar-winning Films
Ben Hur, Titanic, and *Lord of the Rings: Return of the King* gained 11 awards each. *West Side Story* received ten.

4 Actor with Most Oscars–Male
A tie – Walter Brennan, Daniel Day-Lewis, and Jack Nicholson have each won three times.

5 Actor with Most Oscars–Female
Katherine Hepburn, Ingrid Bergman, Frances McDormand, and Meryl Streep have the highest number of Oscar wins.

6 All-time Oscar Winner
Walt Disney – 26 awards.

7 Youngest Oscar Winner
Shirley Temple, who was six years and 310 days old when she won.

8 Oscar Controversy
In 1972, Marlon Brando refused the Best Actor award to protest the US government's mistreatment of Indigenous peoples. He was represented by activist Sacheen Littlefeather.

9 Oscar Venues
The Hollywood Roosevelt Hotel, Ambassador Hotel, Shrine Auditorium, Pantages Theatre, and The Dolby (current) all once hosted the ceremony.

10 Oscar Parties
The official post-award Governor's Ball is held in the Ray Dolby Ballroom at Ovation Hollywood.

🔟 Performing Arts Venues

1 Pantages Theatre
MAP Q2 ▪ 6233 Hollywood Blvd ▪ 323-468-1770 ▪ www.hollywoodpantages.com

This Art Deco jewel *(see p12)* has been restored to its 1929 glory. Once a movie palace, its eye-popping auditorium hosted the Academy Awards from 1949–59.

Walt Disney Concert Hall auditorium

2 Walt Disney Concert Hall
This Frank Gehry creation *(see p48)*, the newest part of the Music Center, features cleverly designed seating that makes listening to the LA Philharmonic Orchestra beneath the sail-like ceiling *(see p78)* an unforgettable experience.

3 Music Center
MAP V4 ▪ 135 N Grand Ave, Downtown ▪ 213-972-7211

This three-venue arts center represents LA culture. The LA Opera, led by conductor James Conlon, makes its home at the Dorothy Chandler Pavilion, while cutting-edge plays are presented at the Ahmanson Theater and the Mark Taper Forum.

4 Ford Amphitheatre
MAP P1 ▪ 2580 Cahuenga Blvd E ▪ 323-850-2000 ▪ www.theford.com

Built in 1920 and embraced by the Hollywood Hills, this intimate outdoor amphitheater presents a multicultural program of music, dance, film, and theater.

5 Greek Theatre
MAP D2 ▪ 2700 N Vermont Ave ▪ 844-524-7335 ▪ www.greektheatrela.com

Tucked into a hillside in Griffith Park, the popular Greek Theatre *(see p34)* has featured such musical greats as B. B. King. The theater's performance season runs from May through October.

6 Theatricum Botanicum
MAP B2 ▪ 1419 N Topanga Canyon Blvd ▪ 310-455-3723 ▪ www.theatricum.com

This theater venue was the brainchild of Will Geer, best known for his portrayal of Grandpa in the 1970s TV series *The Waltons*.

7 Hollywood Bowl
Concerts beneath the stars at this natural amphitheater *(see p100)* are a summer tradition. The range extends from Beethoven and The Beatles to cabaret and rock. Enjoy a picnic before the show. Cheap tickets are available for some shows.

Fireworks display, Hollywood Bowl

The exterior of the Dolby Theatre

⑧ Dolby Theatre
MAP P2 ■ 6801 Hollywood Blvd ■ 323-308-6300 ■ Hourly tours: book online ■ Adm ■ www.dolby theatre.com

Home of the Academy Awards since 2002, this is a stunning venue with a five-level lobby and a grand spiral staircase. Dolby 3-D video imaging and advanced audio technology add to the enjoyment.

⑨ Royce Hall
MAP C2 ■ UCLA Campus, Westwood ■ 310-825-2101 ■ www. roycehall.org

One of UCLA's original buildings, the 1929 Romanesque Royce Hall (see p116) once hosted greats such as George Gershwin. Today, the hall presents an avant-garde calendar of dance, music, and theater events.

⑩ Peacock Theater
MAP S6 ■ 777 Chick Hearn Court ■ 213-763-6030 ■ www. peacocktheater.com

This venue presents concerts on the largest indoor stage in Southern California. The theater also hosts awards shows such as the Primetime Emmys.

TOP 10 COMEDY CLUBS

1 HaHa Comedy Club
4712 Lankershim Blvd
■ 818-508-4995
This club nurtures budding comics.

2 The Groundlings Theatre
7307 Melrose Ave ■ 323-934-4747
TV star Lisa Kudrow (of the TV series *Friends*) graduated from here.

3 The Hollywood Improv
8162 Melrose Ave ■ 323-651-2583
Robin Williams tickled funny bones at this famous haunt with a restaurant.

4 Dynasty Typewriter
2511 Wishire Blvd ■ 657-222-6147
Top-notch alternative comedy talents perform and record podcasts here.

5 Comedy Store
8433 Sunset Blvd ■ 323-650-6268
A legendary club that launched the careers of Jim Carrey and Michael Keaton.

6 Largo at the Coronet
366 N La Cienega ■ www.largo-la.com
This nightclub and cabaret attracts A-list comedians and storytellers.

7 Flappers
102 E Magnolia Blvd, Burbank
■ 818-845-9721
Enjoy dinner and a live comedy show (or two) daily at this location.

8 The Comedy & Magic Club
1018 Hermosa Ave, Hermosa Beach
■ 310-372-1193
Famous comics including Jay Leno (on most Sundays) test new material here.

9 The Ice House
24 N Mentor Ave, Pasadena
■ 626-414-2386
It is one of the US's oldest comedy clubs.

10 The Laugh Factory
8001 Sunset Blvd ■ 323-656-1336
It features big name acts and promising newcomers of all ethnic backgrounds.

The Laugh Factory at Sunset Blvd

🔟 Restaurants

Water Grill, with upscale decor and some of the best seafood in LA

① Water Grill

A premier seafood joint, this place *[see p83]* is usually packed with patrons appreciative of the dock-fresh fare and superb service. Chef Jesse Riofir turns each dish into a celebration of bold flavors and pleasing textures. The white clam chouder and hand-cut tuna tartare are outstanding, and the oyster bar scores high with the pre-theater crowd.

② N/naka

MAP D2 ■ 3455 Overland Ave ■ www.n-naka.com ■ $$$$

The wait for reservations at N/naka is as long as three months – for good reason. The tasting menu is a three-hour experience of 13 exquisitely

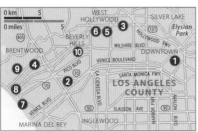

Sea urchin, Providence

presented dishes, which are a modern take on the *kaiseki* (a multi-course Japanese dinner) tradition. Specialties are spaghetti with shaved black abalone and Tasmanian Sea trout tartare with asparagus butter and nasturtium leaf.

③ Providence

MAP Q4 ■ 5955 Melrose Ave, Hollywood ■ www. providencela.com ■ $$$$

Providence serves some of the West Coast's best wild-caught, seafood, fresh from American and international waters. From the series of separate, dining areas, choose the intimate patio room if you are in search of a romantic evening. Fresh truffles are a specialty, as are the changing tasting menus and wine pairings.

④ Echigo

Fine, imaginatively presented sushi of all types is the only offering at this restaurant *[see p113]*. The ambience is simple and plain, with only 12 seats at the L-shaped bar and service is attentive. The *omakase* (chef's choice) is outstanding.

5 Matsuhisa

This (see p119) is the original of a small chain of restaurants serving Nobu Matsuhisa's inspired Japanese-Peruvian fusion fare. The sushi is impeccable and the tempura extra-light, but the chef's talent really lies in cooked seafood dishes, many paired with Nobu's perky sauces. Celebrity sightings are likely. Make reservations several days in advance to avoid the rush.

6 Spago Beverly Hills

A favorite with the rich and famous (see p119) and a great place to sample California cuisine. The menu pairs supreme cuts of meat or fish with seasonal side dishes such as chanterelle mushrooms. The lox pizza is always popular. Early reservations essential.

7 Pasjoli

This Santa Monica bistro (see p127) has a true Parisian vibe, with seasonal local produce starring in a changing homage to traditional French cuisine. Award-winning chef Dave Beran's specialties include a sublime pressed duck breast, steak au poivre, butter-poached lobster in puff pastry, and bitter chocolate soufflé with home-made vanilla ice cream and warm chocolate sauce, all complemented by a fine selection of wines.

Chef Dave Beran, Pasjoli

Alfresco dining at Michael's

8 Michael's

Michael's (see p127) serves Oscar-worthy cuisine in a luscious garden setting, making it one of the best alfresco dining spots in all LA. The food delights both the eye and palate. The decor harks back to its 1979 opening, but a new chef has brought contemporary tastes and ingredients to the menu.

9 Mélisse

Consistently ranked as the top food spot in LA, Josiah Citrin's two-Michelin-starred Mélisse (see p127) uses fresh local ingredients to create classic French cuisine with a modern twist. Seasonal white truffle and game menus also feature. Renovation has turned the restaurant into a 14-seat tasting menu-only experience, making this a top choice for memorable dinners.

10 Maude

You must reserve online over a month in advance to dine at Australian celebrity chef Curtis Stone's unassuming restaurant (see p119). Named after Stone's paternal grandmother, Maude has only 24 seats, an intimate and cozy atmosphere, and an incredibly friendly service. It is set up like a Chef's table where a different ingredient is featured every three months – pistachios, black truffles, or pomegranates, are a few examples – and a ten-course meal is derived from there. Each tasting menu also focuses on one of four of the world's top wine regions.

For a key to restaurant price ranges see p83

TOP 10 Shopping Streets

1 Third Street Promenade
A carnival atmosphere reigns on this popular pedestrian-only strip (see p121), especially during the summer months. Upscale chains such as Club Monaco and Anthropologie dominate, with a few bookstores and old-timers including the Puzzle Zoo toy store thrown in.

2 Montana Avenue
MAP B3 ■ Between 7th & 17th Sts, Santa Monica
You're likely to bump into celebrities in the upscale boutiques on Montana Avenue. It's fun peeking at the clothes, home furnishings, beauty products, and exercise gear favored by fashionistas.

3 Old Town Pasadena
Once a crumbling historic district, Old Town Pasadena (see p93) was given a makeover in the 1990s. Today, Colorado Boulevard and its side streets offer pleasant shopping in mostly mid-priced chains and specialty stores.

4 Rodeo Drive
A stroll along this fabled Los Angeles shopping street (see p115) is a must. All the big names in haute couture have staked out their turf on Rodeo (see p118), including Ralph Lauren, Armani, Balenciaga, Valentino, Dolce & Gabbana, Chanel, and Versace. For better prices, walk just a mile northeast to Beverly Drive.

Shopping on Robertson Boulevard

5 Robertson Boulevard
MAP L5 ■ Between 3rd St & Beverly Blvd
Price tags are steep at the boutiques on this ultracool two-block stretch, but you may be browsing next to celebrities such as Cameron Diaz or Jennifer Aniston. Part of the mix are cutting-edge LA designers.

6 Melrose Avenue
Tattooed 20-somethings buy vintage clothing and jewelry in stores between La Brea Boulevard and Fairfax Avenue (see p112). West of Fairfax is a designer enclave and the Pacific Design Center (see p109) is more about trendy home furnishings.

The upmarket Rodeo Drive

ONE WAY

⑦ Main Street, Santa Monica

A laid-back yet sophisticated string of one-of-a-kind boutiques (with the odd chain store thrown in), Main Street (see p125) makes for a fun shopping and dining experience with plenty of exciting restaurants. On Sundays, catch the farmers' market.

⑧ Abbot Kinney Boulevard
MAP B5 ▪ Between Venice Blvd & Main St

The pint-sized stores here teem with character, not to mention characters. This is Venice, after all: laid-back, hip, and plenty artistic. Fans of 1950s furniture, New Agers in search of aura-enhancing elixirs, and gift shoppers will find all that they want.

Shops at the famed Santee Alley

⑨ Santee Alley
MAP T6 ▪ Between Olympic Blvd & 12th St, Downtown

Bargain hunters will love this pedestrian-only lane, the busiest in the Fashion District and the center of LA's garment industry. In a setting reminiscent of an old bazaar, vendors hawk cut-rate clothing, accessories, and luggage. Alas, fakes are not uncommon, so beware.

⑩ West Third Street
MAP M5 ▪ Between La Cienega Blvd & Fairfax Ave, W Hollywood

Between the Beverly Center and the Original Farmers Market, this shopping strip is a mile-long and is one of the hippest in LA. The bounty ranges from home and jewelry store items to vintage finds and trendy fashions at Polka Dots & Moonbeams.

TOP 10 SHOPPING MALLS

Shops at Santa Monica Place

1 Santa Monica Place
MAP B3 ▪ 310-260-8333
Frank Gehry-designed mall with great food courts.

2 Beverly Center
MAP L5 ▪ 310-854-0070
Upscale retail assortment within a fortress-like facade.

3 The Grove at Farmers Market
323-900-8000
Outdoor mall with mock streetscape and fountains (see p107).

4 Glendale Galleria
MAP D1 ▪ 818-459-4184
Dedicated mall-crawlers will love the 250 mostly mid-priced stores.

5 South Coast Plaza
MAP G4 ▪ 714-435-8571
Over 250 boutiques have made this mall – one of the largest in the US – an international shopping destination.

6 Westfield Century City
MAP C2 ▪ 310-277-3898
Elegant shopping area with boutiques and valet parking.

7 The Paseo
MAP E1 ▪ 626-795-8891
Trendy Pasadena "urban village" with 50 stores, a movie theater, a Hyatt Place hotel and condos.

8 Ovation Hollywood
MAP P2 ▪ 323-467-6412
Choose between the 20-odd stores and restaurants beneath the Hollywood Sign at this outdoor mall (see p13).

9 Westfield Fashion Square
MAP C1 ▪ 818-783-0550
Indoor mall that prides itself on outstanding service.

10 FigAt7th
MAP T5 ▪ 213-955-7150
Fun architecture, great food, and a colorful farmers' market on Thursdays.

TOP 10 Los Angeles for Free

The famous Hollywood Sign in Hollywood Hills

1 Hike to the Hollywood Sign
www.hollywoodsign.org
Protected by a fence and security cameras, the famous 45-ft- (14-m-) tall aluminum letters cannot be reached, but you can get pretty close. Three trails wind upwards through native chaparral, home to abundant wildlife – chickadees and hawks, and occasional deer. Trails are graded easy to difficult, and vary in distance from 3–6.5 miles (5–10.5 km).

2 Downtown Art Walk
www.downtownartwalk.org
Galleries and art exhibitions on Spring and Main between 2nd and 9th streets are open during regular hours, letting anyone walk in and browse the exhibits.

3 Griffith Observatory
Visiting the grounds and iconic Art Deco-style observatory (see pp34–5) are free to the public. City views are spectacular. Stargaze through the Zeiss telescope on a clear night or wonder at a Foucault

The iconic Griffith Observatory

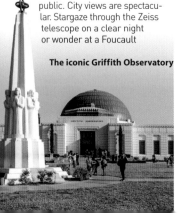

pendulum. Free public star parties are held monthly. There is no charge for parking.

4 Be in the Audience of a TV Show
www.on-camera-audiences.com
Free tickets to your favorite comedy, game, and talk shows are usually distributed on a first-come, first-served basis. Tickets to the more popular shows go fast, so it is advised to reserve in advance. If you are wandering around the Farmers Market or Grove shopping center, you may be approached to fill a seat at the nearby CBS Studio.

Aquarium, California Science Center

5 California Science Center
Free permanent exhibitions feature lots of hands-on activities. Examine an astronaut's suit; learn how bodily organs work together, and explore an underwater kelp forest and polar research station. This (see p86) is a great place for kids of all ages.

6 The Getty Center
This (see pp16–19) is one of LA's great community draws, offering fantastic city-wide views, art exhibitions, gardens, tours, and lectures. Many live musical performances are free too. You only pay for parking, but LA Metro buses stop right at the entrance.

Exhibit at the La Brea Tar Pits Museum

⑦ La Brea Tar Pits

5801 Wilshire Blvd ▪ 323-857-6300 ▪ www.tarpits.org

You can wander around the tar pits and the life-size prehistoric animal models, and contemplate the 40,000 years of hot bubbling asphalt without charge, but paid admission is required for the adjacent museum and its impressive fossil collection.

⑧ Hollywood Bowl Free Rehearsals

During the summer on Tuesday, Thursday, and some Friday mornings from 9am to noon, you can sit in the historic bowl (see p100) and watch rehearsals. The outdoor setting is gorgeous, so bring a picnic lunch. The adjacent Hollywood Bowl Museum is also free.

⑨ Visit Gravesites of the Stars

www.seeing-stars.com/buried

The final resting places of famous movie stars are located across the LA area. Hollywood Forever hands out a map to help you find your favorite celebrity. All are open to the public.

⑩ Free Music Concerts at LACMA

www.lacma.org

LACMA (see pp20–23) sponsors free one-hour concerts every weekend. From April to November, you'll hear jazz on Friday nights and classical on Sundays. Concerts start at 5 or 6pm. From June to August, on Saturday evenings, it's Latin music. Check the website for venues and virtual events.

TOP 10 BUDGET TIPS

1 Free Museum Days
Many museums that are free one day a week or once a month.

2 Theater Tickets
www.theatreinla.com
Get half-price theater tickets for selected plays through Theatre in LA.

3 Go Los Angeles Pass
www.gocity.com
A 1- to 7-day pass to nearly 30 attractions, museums, and tours.

4 Shop at Farmers' Markets
Put together a picnic of reasonably priced fresh, local food from outdoor markets located throughout LA.

5 Happy Hour
On late weekday afternoons, many restaurants offer discounted menu items in the bar area.

6 Senior discounts
Senior citizens qualify for substantial discounts on transportation, museum admissions, movies, and Hollywood Bowl concerts.

7 Get Rid of the Rental Car at Disneyland
If staying multiple days, you don't need a car. Anaheim hotels run free or low-cost shuttles to Disneyland.

8 Save on Parking
Selected lots at Metro Rail and Metrolink stations have free parking for transit users.

9 Disney Tickets
Credit unions, teacher unions, and the Auto Club sometimes offer slightly discounted tickets. Never buy a partly used pass from anybody.

10 Save on Gas
GasBuddy (www.gasbuddy.com) has up-to-date prices for all local gas stations.

ARCO gas station

ⓘⓞ Drives and Day Trips

① Mulholland Drive
MAP C1

Named after William Mulholland, the architect of the Los Angeles aqueduct, this quintessential LA road winds for about 25 miles (40 km) along a Santa Monica Mountains ridge from Hollywood to the western San Fernando Valley. On clear days, the panoramic views over Los Angeles county are truly stunning.

② Mission San Gabriel Arcangel
MAP E2 ▪ 428 S Mission Dr, San Gabriel ▪ 626-457-3035 ▪ Open 8am–4pm Tue–Sun ▪ Adm

Heavy flooding forced the fourth of the California missions to move here five years after it was founded in 1771. Like other Spanish missions in California, it was built by enslaved Indigenous peoples, who had lived on the land for centuries. The mission features a small museum.

Mission San Fernando Rey de España

④ Mission San Fernando Rey de España
15151 San Fernando Mission Blvd, Mission Hills ▪ 818-361-0186 ▪ Open 9am–4:30pm daily ▪ Adm

The 17th of the 21 missions founded by Franciscans in California, San Fernando was established in 1797 to supply food for El Pueblo de Los Angeles. The mission church is an exact replica of the original, destroyed in the 1971 Sylmar earth-quake. The adjacent *convento* (living quarters) is the state's largest surviving adobe structure.

Knott's Berry Farm entrance

③ Knott's Berry Farm
8039 Beach Blvd, Buena Park ▪ 714-220-5200 ▪ Opening hours vary, check website ▪ www.knotts.com

The first theme park in the US, Old West-themed Knott's Berry Farm is known for its gut-wrenching roller coasters. Teens love the Xcelerator and the Supreme Scream, while Camp Snoopy charms younger children. Five themed areas offer entertainment for all ages.

⑤ Six Flags Magic Mountain
26101 Magic Mountain Parkway, Valencia ▪ 661-255-4104 ▪ Opening hours vary, check website ▪ Adm ▪ www.sixflags.com

The Holy Grail for roller-coaster fans, Six Flags has more ways to catapult, spin, loop, spiral, and twist than you or your stomach can imagine. Favorite white-knuckle rides include X2, the world's first four-dimensional coaster, and Superman: Escape from Krypton, which has you free-falling for 6.5 seconds.

6 Santa Barbara and Wine Country

On Hwy 101, about 90 miles (145 km) north of LA

This town, with its Spanish-style architecture and villa-studded hillsides, is quite charming. Apart from the mission building and historical adobes, it is also a must visit for wine connoisseurs. Head for the tasting rooms of the wine country around Santa Ynez, a 45-minute drive away.

7 Queen Mary

MAP E4 ■ 1126 Queen Hwy, Long Beach ■ 562-435-3510 ■ Opening hours vary, check website ■ Adm ■ www.queenmary.com

The *Queen Mary* has whisked as many as 15,000 soldiers per trip from the USA to Europe during World War II. Retired in 1964, she became a tourist attraction three years later. Much of the Queen Mary, which also contains a hotel, can be explored on self-guided tours.

8 Ventura and Channel Islands National Park

On Hwy 101, about 65 miles (105 km) north of LA

Ventura's Main Street is a fun place to browse antiques and second-hand stores. A look inside the Mission San Buenaventura is worthwhile. The town is the gateway to the Channel Islands National Park. Excursions to the islands leave from Ventura Harbor year-round.

9 Nixon Presidential Library and Museum

18001 Yorba Linda Blvd, Yorba Linda ■ 714-993-3393 ■ Open 10am–5pm daily ■ Adm ■ www.nixonlibrary.gov

This memorial to the 37th US president (1913–94) includes a museum, lush gardens, and the restored 1910 farmhouse where he was born. Exhibits focus on Nixon's achievements, but also include a gallery about Watergate. A re-creation of the Lincoln Sitting Room is a highlight.

10 Ronald Reagan Presidential Library and Museum

40 Presidential Dr, Simi Valley ■ 800-410-8354 ■ Open 10am–5pm daily ■ Adm ■ www.reaganlibrary.net

A chunk of the Berlin Wall and a re-created Oval Office are the highlights of this museum devoted to the 40th US president (1911–2004). Exhibits trace Reagan's life from his childhood, through his Hollywood career to his political ascent.

Ventura and Channel Islands National Park

Los Angeles
Area by Area

The Griffith Observatory overlooking
Downtown Los Angeles

TOP 10 Downtown

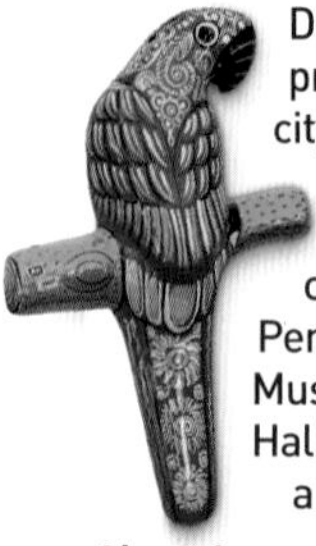

Downtown LA is a microcosm of the city's past, present, and future. El Pueblo commemorates the city's Spanish origins, while Chinatown and Little Tokyo are vibrant communities. The city's financial center, along Flower and Figueroa streets, sits in sharp contrast to the early 20th-century architecture around Pershing Square. Cultural sites include the renowned Museum of Contemporary Art, the Walt Disney Concert Hall, and the galleries of the Arts District. The Fashion and Jewelry districts also add their own flair, and Downtown is dominated by L.A. Live, a vast sports and entertainment district.

Olvera Street souvenir

DOWNTOWN

1 Top 10 Sights
see pp77–9

1 Places to Eat
see p83

1 The Best of the Rest
see p80

1 Public Art
see p82

1 Downtown Architecture
see p81

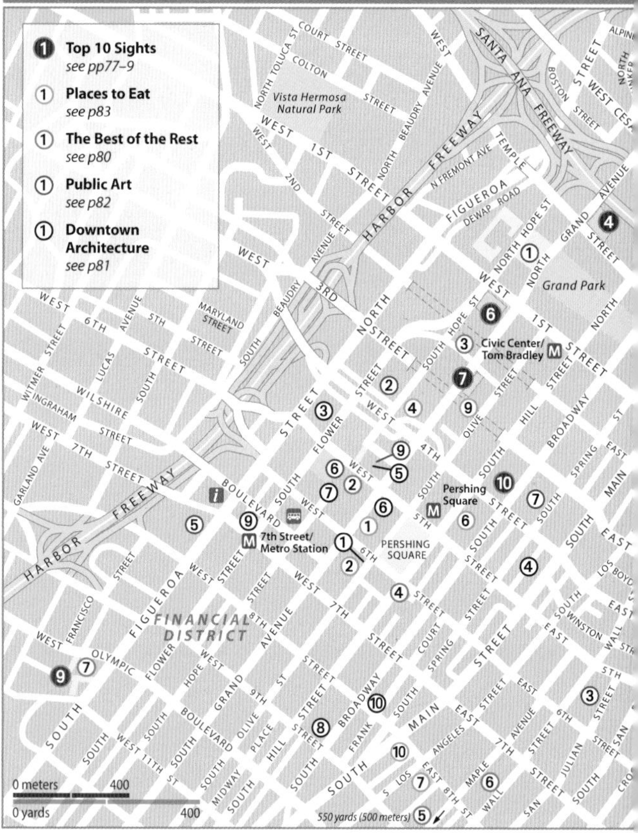

1 El Pueblo de Los Angeles

This historic district *(see pp24–5)* near LA's 1781 founding site comprises buildings dating back to the early 19th century, when the city was just an outpost under Mexican rule. Its main artery, Olvera Street, was restored in the 1930s to a lively lane lined with Mexican trinket shops and restaurants.

2 Union Station
MAP X4 ▪ 800 N Alameda St

Built in 1939 during the rise in popularity of railroad travel, Union Station blends traditional Spanish Mission elements with Modernist Art

One of Union Station's grand halls

Deco touches. Its lofty main waiting room is graced with a coffered wooden ceiling, highly polished marble floors, and tall arched windows. Union Station has been featured in several movies, *The Hustler* (1961) and *Bugsy* (1991) among others.

3 City Hall
MAP W4 ▪ 200 N Spring St
▪ Open 9am–5pm Mon–Fri

This was LA's tallest building for over four decades, with the central tower of this 1928 complex three times higher than the height limit at that time. Renovations have made it possible for the public to admire its marble-columned rotunda once again. City Hall has been immortalized on celluloid countless times, most famously as the headquarters of the *Daily Planet* in the *Superman* TV series. It was also attacked by Martians in *The War of the Worlds* (1953).

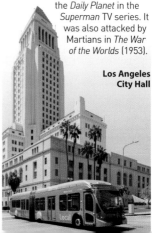

Los Angeles City Hall

4 Cathedral of Our Lady of the Angels

MAP V3 ■ 555 W Temple St ■ 213-680-5200 ■ Open 6am–6pm Mon–Fri, 9am–6pm Sat, 7am–6pm Sun ■ Free tours: hours vary, call ahead ■ www.olacathedral.org

LA's strikingly modern Roman Catholic cathedral looms above the Hollywood Freeway. Enter through giant bronze doors cast by LA sculptor Robert Graham and guarded by a statue of Our Lady of the Angels. The interior of the cathedral is bathed in a soft light that streams in through the alabaster windows.

5 Little Tokyo

MAP W5 ■ Bounded by 1st & 4th, Alameda, & Los Angeles Sts

Japanese communities have lived in LA since the 1880s, but redevelopment in the 1960s saw much of Little Tokyo become home to bland modern architecture. The surviving buildings on East First Street are now a National Historic Landmark. Stop at the Japanese American National Museum, and check out the MOCA Geffen Contemporary (see p80).

6 Walt Disney Concert Hall

MAP V4 ■ 111 S Grand Ave ■ 323-850-2000 ■ www.laphil.com

A spectacular addition to Downtown's landscape is the home of the Los Angeles Philharmonic Orchestra. Frank Gehry conceived the dramatic auditorium (see p64), rather like the sculptural interpretation of a ship at sea. The exterior "sails" are clad in stainless-steel panels, while the hall itself (see p48) boasts a curved wooden ceiling with superb acoustics.

Art exhibit at MOCA

7 Museum of Contemporary Art (MOCA)

MAP U4 ■ 250 S Grand Ave ■ 213-626-6222 ■ Opening hours vary, check website ■ Adm ■ www.moca.org

An early player in Downtown's cultural renaissance, MOCA collects and displays contemporary art in all media from 1940 to the present. The museum was established in 1979 and the building was designed by the famous Japanese architect Arata Isozaki. Works by Jackson Pollock, Andy Warhol, and Roy Lichtenstein form part of its permanent collection.

8 Chinatown

MAP W2 ■ Along Broadway Hill north of Cesar Chavez Blvd

The Chinese first settled in LA after the Gold Rush, but were forced by the construction of Union Station to relocate a few blocks north to an area that was once known as "New Chinatown." A cultural hub with over 20,000 Chinese Americans, this prime shopping district sells everything from fun art to food.

Colorful buildings of Chinatown

CHUNG KING ROAD GALLERIES

This quiet, lantern-festooned lane in western Chinatown is the hotbed of LA's art scene. Artists' studios and several contemporary art galleries have replaced the traditional Chinese antique and furniture stores in the area. Follow a browsing session with a quiet drink at the Chinese Friends restaurant.

 L.A. Live Sports and Entertainment District

MAP S6

A 4,000,000-sq-ft (371,600-sq-m) development, adjoining the Crypto. com Arena and the Los Angeles Convention Center, houses LA's premier sports and entertainment district. Venues include the Peacock Theater, with state-of-the-art acoustics and seating for 7,200 people, and The Novo, a live music venue. At the heart of the center is Microsoft Square.

Grand Central Market

Grand Central Market

MAP V5 ■ 317 S Broadway
■ 213-624-2378 ■ Open 8am–9pm daily ■ www.grandcentralsquare.com

Angelenos have perused the produce aisles of this lively market since 1917. Today, visitors flock here to dine at the city's hippest food stalls for restorative breakfast sandwiches, light lunches, and comforting dinners. Many of the stalls also have long traditions, such as Roast-to-Go, where the Penilla family has served tacos and burritos since the 1950s. The architect Frank Lloyd Wright once had an office upstairs.

A DAY IN DOWNTOWN

▶ MORNING

Begin your day with the historic **El Pueblo** (see p77), which will take you back to the city's vibrant Mexican and Spanish past. Browse colorful **Olvera Street** (see p24) for authentic crafts and food, and then cross Alameda Street for a close-up of the grand **Union Station** (see p77).

Next, go west along Cesar E. Chavez Avenue, before turning right on Broadway for a stroll through **Chinatown** and a superb lunch at the **Philippe's the Original** (see p83).

AFTERNOON

Ride the DASH bus "B" from Broadway to Temple Street, dominated by the **Cathedral of Our Lady of the Angels**. After admiring Rafael Moneo's Modernist masterpiece, head south along Grand Avenue, past the **Music Center** (see p64) and the **Walt Disney Concert Hall** to check out the latest exhibits at the **MOCA**.

Stroll down **Bunker Hill Steps** (see p81), stopping to gaze at *Source Figure*, Robert Graham's exquisite sculpture and the **Central Library** (see p80). Walk to Pershing Square, lorded over by the baronial **Millennium Biltmore Hotel** (see p81), a nice place for tea or coffee. Leave in time to make it to the Victorian **Bradbury Building** (see p49) before 5pm. Browse for treasures in the bountiful aisles of the **Grand Central Market**.

See map on pp76–7 ←

The Best of the Rest

1 Row DTLA
MAP W6 ▪ 777 S. Alameda
▪ www.rowdtla.com

This garment factory complex in downtown LA has become a hotspot for creative boutiques, high fashion shops, and street food.

2 Central Library
MAP U5 ▪ 630 W 5th St ▪ 213-228-7000 ▪ Open 10am–8pm Mon–Thu, 9:30am–5:30pm Fri–Sat, 1–5pm Sun

LA's main library consists of the original 1926 building, a Beaux-Arts design by Bertram Goodhue, and an art-filled atrium added in 1993.

Reading room, Central Library

3 The Broad
MAP V4 ▪ 221 S Grand Ave
▪ 213-622-6200 ▪ Opening hours vary, check website ▪ www.the broad.org

A superb contemporary art collection housed in a striking building. Yayoi Kusama's dazzling *Infinity Mirrored Room* is especially popular.

4 Jewelry District
MAP U5 ▪ Hill St just off Pershing Square

Precious gems, watches, and fine jewels are sold in shops in what has long been the center of Los Angeles's jewelry industry.

5 Fashion District
MAP U6 ▪ Bounded by Broadway, San Pedro St, 7th St, & 16th St

The 56-block district (see p69) is the heart of LA's clothing industry and heaven on earth for bargain hunters.

6 The Original LA Flower Market
MAP V6 ▪ 754 Wall St
▪ 213-627-3696 ▪ Opening hours vary, check website ▪ Adm ▪ www. originallaflowermarket.com

This 1913 cut-flower market, the largest in the country, has it all from roses to orchids.

7 The GRAMMY Museum
MAP S6 ▪ 800 W Olympic Blvd
▪ 213-725-5700 ▪ Open 11am–5pm Wed–Mon, 10am–6pm Sat ▪ www. grammymuseum.org

You can record and perform a song at this interactive museum dedicated to the music industry.

8 Japanese American National Museum
MAP W5 ▪ 100 N Central Ave
▪ 213-625-0414 ▪ Open 11am–5pm Tue, Wed & Fri–Sun, noon–8pm Thu ▪ Adm ▪ www.janm.org

Formerly housed in a Buddhist temple, this museum chronicles the history of Japanese Americans.

9 MOCA Geffen Contemporary
MAP W5 ▪ 152 N Central Ave
▪ 213-626-6222 ▪ Opening hours vary, check website ▪ www.moca.org

This huge former police garage hosts traveling shows and exhibits.

10 Downtown Arts District
MAP U4 ▪ Bounded by 1st & 7th Sts, Alameda Ave, & the Los Angeles River

Public art murals, trendy galleries, shops, and restaurants are abundant in this vibrant neighborhood.

Downtown Architecture

1 ## Oviatt Building
MAP U5 ■ 617 S Olive St

This 1927 Art Deco gem *(see p83)* has French fixtures and a forecourt decorated with Lalique glass. It houses the popular Cicada restaurant.

2 ## Coca-Cola Bottling Plant
MAP E3 ■ 1334 S Central Ave
■ **Closed to the public**

A Streamline Moderne building, located in an industrial area, this resembles an ocean liner, complete with porthole windows. Drive past it on your way to the highway for full effect.

3 ## Westin Bonaventure Hotel & Suites
MAP U4 ■ 404 S Figueroa St
■ **213-624-1000**

The five mirror-glass cylinders of LA's biggest hotel *(see p148)* look like a space ship ready for take-off.

4 ## Old Bank District
MAP V5 ■ On 4th St between Main & Spring Sts

This trio of statuesque buildings, built between 1904 and 1910, has been converted into residential lofts.

5 ## US Bank Tower
MAP U5 ■ 633 W 5th St

Standing at 1,017 ft (310 m), this building was erected only after developers were forced to purchase the air rights from neighboring Central Library in order to exceed official height limits.

US Bank Tower skyscraper

Interior of Millennium Biltmore Hotel

6 ## Millennium Biltmore Hotel
MAP U5 ■ 506 S Grand Ave
■ **213-624-1011**

A range of architectural styles, from Renaissance to Neo-Classical, adorn this 1923 Beaux-Arts hotel.

7 ## Bunker Hill Steps
MAP U4

Cascading from Hope Street to Fifth Street, these steps *(see p82)* have many features, including a sculpture of a female nude by Robert Graham.

8 ## Eastern Columbia Building
MAP U6 ■ 849 Broadway

A bright turquoise terracotta mantle covers this former 1930s furniture and clothing store.

9 ## Fine Arts Building
MAP T5 ■ 811 W 7th St
■ **Open during office hours only**

Behind the richly detailed facade of this 1927 building awaits a galleried lobby in Spanish Renaissance style.

10 ## Broadway Historic Theater District
MAP U6 ■ Along Broadway between 3rd & 9th Sts

During the silent-film era, Broadway was the most popular movie district. The movie palaces here are architectural marvels.

See map on pp76–7 ←

Public Art

1 Peace on Earth
MAP V4 ■ Music Center Plaza, 135 N Grand Ave
Created at the height of the Vietnam War in 1969, Jacques Lipchiz's bronze Madonna has the dove, a symbol of peace, on top, and lambs, representing humanity, at the base.

2 Four Arches
MAP U4 ■ 333 S Hope St
Alexander Calder is best known for his suspended mobiles, but this looming 1975 steel work painted in glowing fiery orange-red is a "stabile," an abstract stationary sculpture.

3 The Heart of Skid Row
MAP V6 ■ Los Angeles Mission 303 East 5th St
Renowned street artist Kenny Scharf's 66-ft (20-m) high mural graces the rounded corner of the LA Mission. The colorful mural is dedicated to alleviating poverty and the homeless crisis in the area.

Peace on Earth

Molecule Man by Jonathan Borofsky

4 Molecule Man
MAP W4 ■ 255 E Temple St
This monumental sculpture by Jonathan Borofsky shows four embracing figures, symbolizing the commonality between people based on their shared molecular structure.

5 Corporate Head
MAP T5 ■ 725 S Figueroa St
An evocative sculpture (1990) by Terry Allen, it condemns the greed and erosion of moral responsibility in today's corporate America.

6 Spine
MAP U4 ■ Maguire Gardens, west side of Central Library, Flower, & 5th Sts
Jud Fine's 1993 installation is a visual allegory of a book – the well symbolizes the title page, the steps the pages, and the pools the plot flow.

7 Biddy Mason: A Passage of Time
MAP V5 ■ 333 S Spring St, near 3rd St
This memorial by Betye Saar and Sheila de Bretteville commemorates the story of former enslaved man Biddy Mason (1818–91), who established the city's first Black church.

8 Astronaut Ellison S. Onizuka Memorial
MAP W5 ■ Onizuka St, Little Tokyo
A 1/10th scale model of the *Challenger*, this 1990 memorial by Isao Hirai honors the first Japanese American astronaut.

9 Source Figure
MAP U4 ■ Hope St, near 4th St
Overlooking the Bunker Hill Steps, *(see p81)* this bronze African American female nude was designed by Robert Graham in 1992. She represents the source of the water cascading down the stairs.

10 Traveler
MAP X4 ■ Union Station
Terry Schoonhoven's 1993 ceramic mural *(see p25)* depicts California travelers from the days of the Spanish explorations, and LA landmarks such as Pico House.

Places to Eat

PRICE CATEGORIES
Price categories include a three-course meal for one, a glass of house wine, and all unavoidable extra charges including tax.

$ under $30 $$ $30–$60 $$$ $60–$90
$$$$ over $90

1 Water Grill
MAP U5 ■ 544 S Grand Ave
■ 213-891-0900 ■ $$$

Fish and seafood fanciers flock to this clubby shrine, which uses impeccably fresh ingredients. Desserts are superb.

2 Cicada
MAP U5 ■ 617 S Olive St
■ 213-488-9488 ■ $$$

The sumptuous Art Deco dining room in the historic Oviatt Building almost overshadows the food. The menu features north Italian classics.

3 Redbird
MAP V5 ■ 114 E 2nd St
■ 213-788-1191 ■ $$$

Set in a former cathedral, Redbird serves California haute cuisine and strong craft cocktails in an airy modern space.

4 Nick & Stef's Steakhouse
MAP U4 ■ 330 S Hope St, Wells Fargo Center ■ 213-680-0330 ■ $$$

Loosen your belt for the juiciest steaks ever. Preview your cut in the glass-encased aging chamber.

5 Yang Chow
MAP W2 ■ 819 N Broadway, Chinatown ■ 213-625-0811 ■ $

In this reliable Chinese restaurant, a plate of the hallmark "slippery shrimp" graces almost every table. The *moo-shu* pork is also a good bet.

6 Perch
MAP U5 ■ 448 S Hill St
■ 213-802-700 ■ $$$

One of the city's most romantic spots, Perch offers rooftop views and a tasty menu of French haute cuisine. The truffle French fries are famous.

7 Sonoratown
MAP U6 ■ 208 E 8th St
■ 213-222-5071 ■ $

Sonora is known for its traditional north Mexican tacos, stuffed with carne asada. The homemade tortillas are some of the best in the city.

The historic deli of Philippe's

8 Philippe the Original
MAP X3 ■ 1001 N Alameda St
■ 213-628-3781 ■ $

Philippe's has served its famous French-dipped sandwiches since 1908. Seating is at long communal tables. Limited vegetarian options.

9 Noe
MAP X4 ■ 251 S Olive St
■ 213-356-4100 ■ $$$$

A romantic place for pre-theater dining, Noe offers fresh seafood, meats, and poultry prepared in an American-Japanese fusion style.

10 Casa La Doña
MAP U6 ■ 800 S Main St
■ 213-627-7441 ■ Open daily, breakfast only Fri–Sun ■ $

A salsa bar with flavorsome regional dishes from Mexico, home-made tortillas, tamales, and spot-on service. Try the fresh blue-gill fish.

See map on pp76–7 ←

TOP 10 Around Downtown

It has been said that LA is not really a city, but a collection of 88 independent towns that overlap. Nowhere is this truer than within the 5-mile (8-km) radius of Downtown. West of here, Koreatown is home to the largest Korean population in the US, while east LA has a large Mexican American population. In the Latino-Byzantine quarter, surrounding St. Sophia Cathedral, Central American and Greek communities predominate. Northwest is Dodger Stadium, a world-famous landmark, while south of the center is Exposition Park with its museums and sports venues.

Hale House, Heritage Square Museum

1 Heritage Square Museum

MAP E2 ■ 3800 Homer St, Highland Park ■ 323-222-3319 ■ Open 11am–5pm Sat–Sun ■ Adm ■ www.heritagesquare.org

Apart from those on Carroll Avenue, most Victorian homes in LA were demolished. A few, however, were moved by helicopter to form the Heritage Square Museum. Eight vintage beauties cluster here, with Hale House, the most outstanding.

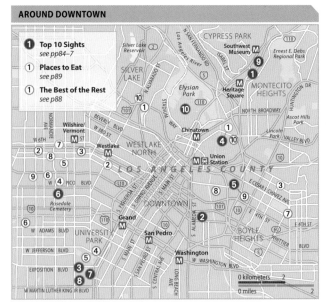

AROUND DOWNTOWN

1 **Top 10 Sights**
see pp84–7

1 **Places to Eat**
see p89

1 **The Best of the Rest**
see p88

Entrance to the San Antonio Winery, the last of its kind in Los Angeles

② Institute of Contemporary Art LA

MAP V6 ■ 7th St ■ 213-928-0833 ■ Opening hours vary, check website ■ www.theicala.org

Founded in 1984 as the Santa Monica Museum of Art, this museum opened at its new location in 2017 and has played a crucial role in the revitalization of downtown. Exhibitions feature contemporary artists from around the world and reflect the cultural diversity and energy of the city. The facility also offers an open-air courtyard and café.

③ Natural History Museum

MAP D3 ■ 900 Exposition Blvd, Exposition Park ■ 213-763-3466 ■ Open 9:30am–5pm daily ■ Adm (free for under 5s) ■ www.nhm.org

Spend a day exploring this engaging museum where the dinosaurs always draw huge crowds, as does the Age of Mammals exhibit with the Simi Valley mastodon, and the 14.5-ft (4-m) long megamouth, the rarest shark in the world. The Gem and Mineral Hall contains a huge gold exhibit and a walk-through gem vault. Cultural exhibits explain and highlight the traditions of Indigenous and Latin American civilizations. Children love the hands-on activities in the Discovery Center and the Insect Zoo.

Quartz gemstone at the Natural History Museum

④ San Antonio Winery

MAP E2 ■ 737 Lamar St, Lincoln Heights ■ 323-223-1401 ■ Tasting room: opening hours vary, call for details ■ www.sanantonio winery.com

LA's only surviving winery *(see p89)* is tucked away in the industrial area north of the Los Angeles River, an area once blanketed with vineyards. When founder Santo Cambianica arrived in 1917, he faced competition from over 100 wineries. Prohibition put most out of business, but Santo survived making sacramental wine. Taste the wines and try the restaurant – a popular lunch spot.

⑤ Mariachi Plaza

MAP Y5 ■ 1831 E First Street

For decades, this colorful open-air plaza is where musicians versed in the Mexican tradition of mariachi wait for their daily gigs (spot them in black velvet suits and large hats as they practice with guitars and horns). With its own metro station and an unmatched daily bustle, Mariachi Plaza is the de facto heart of Boyle Heights' historic Latino community, surrounded by contemporary restaurants, stores, and coffee shops.

The impressive altar and religious iconography at St. Sophia Cathedral

6 St. Sophia Cathedral

MAP D2 ■ 1324 S Normandie Ave, Koreatown ■ 323-737-2424 ■ Open 10am–4pm Tue–Fri, 8:30–1pm Sun ■ www.stsophia.org

One of LA's surprises, this central church of Southern California's Greek Orthodox community is an opulent hall of worship. The eye is drawn to the icon-studded, golden altar of the Virgin Mary, while Jesus, surrounded by saints, looks down at the congregation from the 90-ft (27-m) high dome.

California African American Museum

7 California African American Museum

MAP D2 ■ 600 State Dr, Exposition Park ■ 213-744-7432 ■ Open 10am–5pm Tue–Sat, 11am–5pm Sun ■ Parking $12 ■ www.caamuseum.org

This museum celebrates the art, history, and culture of African Americans, especially in relation to California and the western US. The main exhibit traces the journey from Africa to slavery throughout America to final freedom on the West Coast. Exhibits here highlight the contributions made by African American artists to American culture.

8 California Science Center

MAP D2 ■ 700 Exposition Park Dr, Exposition Park ■ 323-724-3623 ■ Open 10am–5pm daily ■ Parking $15 ■ www.californiasciencecenter.org

Filled with clever and engaging interactive exhibits, this highly entertaining science and technology museum (see p58) has three themed galleries. The World of Life exhibit explains the processes living organisms undergo, Ecosystems demonstrates how everything in nature is connected, and the Air and Space Gallery explores the great beyond. But it's the Space Shuttle *Endeavour* that steals the show and attracts the crowds.

9 Charles F. Lummis Home and Garden

MAP E2 ■ 200 E Ave 43, Highland Park ■ 323-226-1620 ■ Open 10am–3pm Sat–Sun ■ Donation

This was once the home of the eccentric Charles Fletcher Lummis (1859–1928), who walked the entire 3,000 miles (4,830 km) from Ohio to LA in 1885. An

KOREATOWN

Parts of western Vermont Avenue around Wilshire Boulevard west of Downtown would not look out of place in Seoul. These are the main arteries of Koreatown, home to the largest Korean population in the US and a hub of commercial activity. Learn more about the Korean community at the Korean Cultural Center at 5505 Wilshire Blvd.

outspoken California booster and preservationist, Lummis built his house with his own hands out of concrete and found materials, including boulders and railroad rails. The house is also known as El Alisal, Spanish for "sycamore," due to the giant sycamore by the building.

⑩ Dodger Stadium
■ MAP W1 ■ Vin Scully Ave ■ 323-224-1448 ■ Tours (on non-game days by appointment only), tickets required ■ www.dodgers.mlb.com/la/ballpark

For many, spring wouldn't be the same without baseball. The pilgrimage to Dodger Stadium to watch the "Boys in Blue" fight it out is an annual ritual for thousands of fans. Hunkered in the bleachers, munching on the famous Dodger Dogs, they watch the LA Dodgers in action. The stadium opened in 1962 and is often called one of US's most beautiful ballparks. It has hosted the World Series, many concerts, and even a papal mass.

Dodger Stadium on a match day

EXPLORING EXPOSITION PARK IN A DAY

▶ **MORNING**

Start at **Exposition Park** from Figueroa Street and make the **Natural History Museum** (see p85) the first stop of the day. Admire its lovely facade, before delving into the exhibits inside. A landmark bronze sculpture of a *Tyrannosaurus rex* battling a *Triceratops* stands to the north outside. Crossing the street takes you to the **University of Southern California** campus (see p88), where you can join a free guided tour offered hourly from 10am to 3pm (reservations required). Have lunch at the **Mercado La Paloma** (3655 S Grand Ave), a Latin-style community center with colorful crafts stalls and casual eating outlets.

AFTERNOON

Backtrack to Exposition Park and start the afternoon with a look at the **Los Angeles Memorial Coliseum** (3911 S Figueroa St), the main venue of the 1932 and 1984 Olympics. The two huge headless bronze figures outside the eastern entrance were designed by local sculptor Robert Graham. Just north of this spot is the **California Science Center**, with many interactive exhibits. Grab a cold drink from the cafeteria downstairs and head outside to the fragrant **Rose Garden** (see p52) to relax. If you still have the energy left, check out the **California African American Museum**. Otherwise, wind down the day with a 3-D adventure at the **IMAX Theater** (see p62) next to the Science Center.

See map on p84 ←

The Best of the Rest

1 Angelus Temple
MAP E1 ■ 1100 Glendale Blvd, Echo Park ■ Open only during special events

Founded by a popular preacher with a flair for theatrics, this 1923 domed building was once the headquarters of the Foursquare Gospel Church.

2 The Wiltern
MAP D2 ■ 3790 Wilshire Blvd, Koreatown

A live concert venue, encased by the 1931 Art Deco Pellissier Building.

3 Bullocks Wilshire Building
MAP D2 ■ 3050 Wilshire Blvd, Koreatown

One of the earliest Art Deco structures anywhere in the United States, this beautiful building is now home to the Southwestern University School of Law.

4 Shrine Auditorium
MAP D2 ■ 665 W Jefferson Blvd, Exposition Park area

This 1926 Moorish-style theater seats up to 6,300 and was once the largest in the US.

5 University of Southern California (USC)
MAP D2 ■ Bounded by Jefferson, Figueroa, Exposition Blvds & Vermont Ave, Exposition Park area ■ 213-740-2311 ■ www.usc.edu

Built in 1880, the oldest private university in Western US counts George Lucas among its alumni.

6 William Andrews Clark Memorial Library
MAP D2 ■ 2520 Cimarron St, W Adams district ■ 310-794-5155 ■ Tours by appointment

This 1926 building has a rare collection of English books only available to scholars, and an oak-paneled music room.

7 El Mercado de Los Angeles
MAP E2 ■ 3425 E 1st St, E LA ■ 323-262-4507 ■ Open 9am–9pm daily

Stop for a traditional meal or browse colorful stalls at this Mexican-American indoor marketplace.

8 Self Help Graphics & Arts
MAP E2 ■ 1300 E First St, E LA ■ 323-881-6444 ■ Temporarily closed for renovations

This nonprofit arts center works with the Latin American community on print-making, workshops, and exhibitions.

9 Mariachi Plaza
MAP E2 ■ Corner of Boyle Ave & 1st St, E LA

Mariachi musicians in black robes gather in this small park, waiting to be hired for the night's engagements.

10 Brewery Arts Complex
MAP E2 ■ 1920 N Main St, Lincoln Heights ■ 323-222-3007 ■ Opening hours for galleries vary

Art walks are organized twice yearly at this massive artists' colony.

University of Southern California

Places to Eat

① Maddalena Restaurant

MAP E2 ■ 737 Lamar St, Lincoln Heights ■ 323-223-1401 ■ Open 9am–6pm Mon–Thu (to 7pm Fri–Sun) ■ Tours daily ■ $$

This slice of Italy, in what was once the cellars of the San Antonio Winery (see p85), is a popular lunch spot.

Maddalena Restaurant

② Langer's Delicatessen

MAP E2 ■ 704 S Alvarado St ■ 213-483-8050 ■ Closed Sun ■ $

Award-winning Jewish deli serving LA's best pastrami sandwich.

③ El Tepeyac Café

MAP E2 ■ 812 N Evergreen Ave, E LA ■ 323-268-1960 ■ No credit cards ■ $

Long lines form at LA's burrito "head-quarters" for the "Hollenbeck," stuffed with gua-camole and pork.

Burritos, El Tepeyac

④ Papa Cristo's

MAP D2 ■ 2771 W Pico Blvd, Koreatown ■ 323-737-2970 ■ Closed Mon & Tue ■ $

Drop into this friendly, busy restaurant next door to St. Sophia (see p86) for big portions of great Greek food.

⑤ Soot Bull Jeep

MAP D2 ■ 3136 8th St, Koreatown ■ 213-387-3865 ■ Closed Wed ■ $$

Grill your own deliciously marinated meat at this Korean spot.

PRICE CATEGORIES
Price categories include a three-course meal for one, a glass of house wine, and all unavoidable extra charges including tax.

$ under $30 $$ $30–$60 $$$ $60–$90 $$$$ over $90

⑥ Guelaguetza

MAP D2 ■ 3014 W Olympic Blvd, Koreatown ■ 213-427-0601 ■ Closed Mon ■ $

This lively restaurant serving food from southern Mexico is famous for its *moles* – sauces made from spices, nuts, chilies, and chocolate.

⑦ HMS Bounty

MAP D2 ■ 3357 Wilshire Blvd ■ 213-385-7275 ■ $$

Popular historic local hangout with retro chic. Steaks, pub food, and cheap drinks are served up in nautical surroundings. Film shoots take place here once in a while.

⑧ Taylor's Steakhouse

MAP D2 ■ 3361 W 8th St, Koreatown ■ 213-382-8449 ■ $$$

This throwback to the 1950s features faux leather booths and offers huge servings of steak, almost the size of baseball mitts.

⑨ El Cholo

MAP D2 ■ 1121 S Western Ave, Koreatown ■ 323-734-2773 ■ $$

This festive Mexican café has been full of diners hungry for fajitas and burritos since 1923. Their mar-garitas pack a wicked punch.

⑩ Masa of Echo Park

MAP D2 ■ 1800 Sunset Blvd ■ 213-989-1558 ■ Closed Mon & Tue ■ $$

This funky corner café was one of the first in LA to offer the Chicago-style pizza. The wait for their hearty deep-dish pies can be an hour or more so call ahead before visiting.

See map on p84

TOP 10 Pasadena

Pasadena may be considered part of LA, but it is, in fact, distinctly apart. As the city's first suburb, it attracted a large share of the rich, who saw to it that a European flair enhanced the town. Fine mansions, such as the Craftsman-era Gamble House, occupy grounds on leafy streets. Old Town Pasadena, the historic core, is now home to a vibrant street of restaurants and shops. Pasadena is in the limelight every year on January 1 with its Tournament of Roses, a parade, and football game. The area's other treasures include the Rose Bowl and the fabled Huntington Gardens.

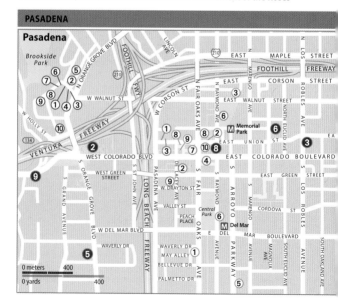

The Rose Bowl, home to the famous annual Tournament of the Roses

1 Rose Bowl

MAP E1 ■ 1001 Rose Bowl Dr ■ 626-577-3101 ■ www.rosebowl stadium.com

Pasadena's most famous landmark, the Rose Bowl, draws worldwide attention every New Year's Day when two top-ranking college football teams battle it out for the Rose Bowl Game Trophy. College football first became part of the Tournament of Roses in 1902 when Michigan beat Stanford 49–0. The original horse-shoe-shaped structure was enlarged to its current capacity of 90,000.

Paintings on display at Norton Simon Museum

2 Norton Simon Museum

MAP E1 ■ 411 W Colorado Blvd ■ 626-449-6840 ■ Open noon–5pm Thu–Mon (until 7pm Fri & Sat) ■ Adm (free for under 19s and students with ID, also on 1st Fri of month) ■ www.nortonsimon.org

This must-see for art lovers owes its existence to Norton Simon, a hugely successful entrepreneur, who collected hundreds of masterpieces *(see p94)* from the Renaissance to the 20th century, and sculptures from India and Southeast Asia. Old Masters, such as Rembrandt and Goya, and the Impressionists, especially Degas, Renoir, Cézanne, and Monet, are well represented. Frank Gehry's remodel improved the lighting of the exhibit space. Sculptures, including a cast of Rodin's *The Thinker*, dot the gardens, inspired by Monet's at Giverny in France.

3 USC Pacific Asia Museum

MAP E1 ■ 46 N Los Robles Ave ■ 626-787-2680 ■ Open 11am–5pm Wed–Sun ■ Adm ■ www.pacificasiamuseum.usc.edu

Grace Nicholson, infatuated with all things Asian, had her home designed to look like a Chinese imperial palace. It now makes a fitting setting for this museum's 15,000 artifacts from Asia and the Pacific Islands. Past exhibitions have included masks from New Guinea, paintings by Japanese masters Hokusai and Hiroshige, and woven costumes from Pakistan.

4 The Huntington

This treasure trove of culture *(see pp28–31)* is the legacy of the railroad tycoon Henry E. Huntington. He made his fortune in real estate and owned LA's first mass transit system.

---

① Top 10 Sights
see pp91–3

① Places to Eat
see p97

① Shopping in Old Pasadena
see p96

① Greene and Greene Craftsman Houses
see p95

Area of main map

North East LA

⑤ Wrigley Mansion and Gardens

MAP E1 ■ 391 S Orange Grove Blvd ■ 626-449-4100 ■ Tours: call ahead for schedule, reservations required

William Wrigley Jr., of Wrigley's chewing gum, certainly knew how to live. His residence in Pasadena is a 18,500-sq-ft (1,720-sq-m) Renaissance-style mansion (see p52). It houses the Tournament of Roses, which organizes the annual Rose Bowl Game. Memorabilia includes Rose Queen crowns, trophies, and photographs.

DOO DAH PARADE

This over-the-top celebration of wackiness, held in mid-November, began in 1978 as an irreverent parody of the wholesome Rose Parade. Entrants vary each year, but groups such as the Synchronized Precision Briefcase Drill Team and the West Hollywood Cheerleaders always generate cheers from the crowd on Colorado Boulevard.

Wrigley Mansion and Gardens

⑥ Pasadena Civic Center

MAP E1 ■ City Hall: 100 N Garfield Ave, 626-744-4000 ■ Civic Auditorium: 300 E Green St, 626-449-7360 ■ Library: closed for renovation until 2025

This grand complex was inspired by the early 20th-century City Beautiful movement. It consists of three European-style Beaux-Arts structures – the Main Library, the Civic Auditorium, and the City Hall. Architect Myron Hunt designed the public library.

⑦ California Institute of Technology (CalTech)

MAP E2 ■ 1200 E California Blvd ■ 626-395-6811 ■ Campus open anytime ■ Free guided tours: hours vary, call ahead ■ www.caltech.edu

One of the world's leading scientific research centers and a pioneer in molecular biology, CalTech counts 46 Nobel Prize winners among its alumni and faculty, including biologist and President Emeritus, David Baltimore. The institute evolved from an arts and crafts school founded in 1891 by the eminent Amos G. Throop, changing its

City Hall, Pasadena Civic Center

focus to science after astronomer George E. Hale became a board member in 1907.

8 Old Town Pasadena
MAP E2 ■ Along Colorado Blvd between Marengo Ave & Pasadena Ave ■ Castle Green, 99 S Raymond Ave

Pasadena's historic business district, once a decaying part of town in the 1900s, has now been beautifully restored. Today, its handsome brick buildings are packed with boutiques, restaurants, and bookstores. A short detour will take you to the imposing Castle Green, once Old Pasadena's most luxurious resort hotel.

9 Colorado Street Bridge
MAP E1 ■ Court ■ 125 S Grand Ave

The arches of this restored 1913 bridge straddle the Arroyo Seco (Spanish for "dry brook"), a ravine that starts in the San Gabriel Mountains. The 1903 Vista del Arroyo Hotel overlooking the bridge is home to the Ninth Circuit Court of Appeals. The local historic group throws a block party on the bridge each July.

Colorado Street Bridge

10 Pasadena Playhouse
MAP E1 ■ 39 S El Molino Ave ■ 626-356-7529 ■ Box office: noon–6pm Tue–Sat (until 4pm Sun) ■ www.pasadenaplayhouse.org

Known as the official state theater of California, it was founded in 1917 and opened in its historic building in 1925. The theater in the round technique was first used here and it has been a center of innovation and a training ground for various artists since. Today it is the center of the Playhouse District of entertainment and shopping.

EXPLORING HISTORIC PASADENA

▶ MORNING

A classic way to start the day in Pasadena is with an energizing breakfast at **Marston's** *(see p97)*. After your fill of pancakes, stroll east a couple of blocks on Walnut Street and have a look at the beautiful Beaux-Arts **Main Library** and the majestic **City Hall** a little to the south. Continue walking farther south to Colorado Boulevard, then head west to **Old Town Pasadena**, the city's original Downtown, a popular shopping and dining district. Check out the well-restored historic facades while browsing the stores, then pause briefly for a snack at **Café Santorini** *(see p97)*.

AFTERNOON

In the afternoon, either drive or walk west along Colorado Boulevard, then turn right on Orange Grove Boulevard to catch the 1pm tour of the **Gamble House** *(see p95)*, the Craftsman-era magnum opus by Charles and Henry Greene. Fans of this architectural style could check out several more residences designed by the brothers along nearby Arroyo Terrace and Grand Avenue. Alternatively, make your way back to Colorado Boulevard for a visit to the first-rate **Norton Simon Museum** *(see p91)*. The gorgeous gardens are a nice place for some respite and refreshments. A perfect finale to your day is to treat yourself to a grand dinner at **The Raymond** *(see p97)*, one of the city's oldest and most popular restaurants.

See map on pp90–91 ←

Artworks at the Norton Simon Museum

① Madonna and Child with Book

Renowned renaissance artist Raphael (1483–1520) was only 19 years old when he painted this work. It perfectly exemplifies his geometrically balanced compositions and his ability to imbue his figures with spirituality and great tenderness.

② Self-Portrait

No artist has left behind such a thorough record of his own likeness as Rembrandt (1606–69). The elegant garb, dapper beret, and gold chain in this portrait emphasize his social status as a sought-after artist.

③ Still Life with Lemons, Oranges, and a Rose

In this still life, Francisco de Zurbarán (1598–1664) applies the bright colors and minute detail usually reserved for his depictions of saints and clergy.

④ Allegory of Virtue and Nobility

Rococo master Giovanni Battista Tiepolo (1696–1770) is known for his exuberant ceiling frescoes. This canvas shows off his bold compositions and use of color.

⑤ Artist's Garden at Vétheuil

Claude Monet (1840–1926) looked out from his house on the Seine at the sunny, flower-filled garden of this painting.

⑥ Little Dancer Aged Fourteen

Edgar Degas (1834–1917) was fascinated with dancers, and this exquisite sculpture is one of his finest. The figure is partly painted, dressed in a tulle skirt, and has been given real hair.

Portrait of a Peasant by Van Gogh

⑦ Portrait of a Peasant

Vincent van Gogh (1853–90) painted Patience Escalier, a gardener and shepherd, against a night-blue background to create "a mysterious effect, like a star in the depths of an azure sky."

⑧ Exotic Landscape

Henri Rousseau (1844–1910) is renowned for his poetic Naïve paintings that depict lushly landscaped dream worlds. He created this work shortly before his death.

⑨ Woman with a Book

A highlight of the museum's extensive Picasso (1881–1973) holdings, this graceful painting shows the artist's mistress, Marie-Thérèse Walter, in an introspective mood that contrasts sharply with the melodramatic colors.

⑩ Leaf In The Wind

Agnes Martin (1912–2004) was most influential in the Abstract Expressionism movement and a leader in Minimalism. This large work shows her skill at portraying pure form with a delicate touch.

Little Dancer Aged Fourteen by Degas

Craftsman Houses by Greene and Greene

1 Van Rossem-Neill House (1903)
MAP E1 ■ 400 Arroyo Terrace

Hemmed in by an unusual wall made of warped clinker bricks, this pretty house has a stained-glass front door.

2 Cole House (1906)
MAP E1 ■ 2 Westmoreland Place

This large home, owned by a church, marks the first time the Greenes added a *porte-cochère* (a porch-like roof) above the driveway.

3 Ranney House (1907)
MAP E1 ■ 440 Arroyo Terrace

Mary Ranney was a draftsperson at the brothers' firm and contributed many of the design ideas for this shingled corner mansion.

4 F. W. Hawks House (1906)
MAP E1 ■ 408 Arroyo Terrace

This home is distinguished by a very wide covered porch, which keeps out both heat and light, giving the house a rather sombre appearance.

5 Gamble House (1908)
MAP E1 ■ 4 Westmoreland Place ■ 626-793-3334 ■ Tour hours vary, check website ■ Adm (free for under 12s) ■ www.gamblehouse.org

This handcrafted masterpiece *(see p49)* features rich wood, leaded glass windows, and a stained-glass door.

The Gamble House

6 White Sisters House (1903)
MAP E1 ■ 370 Arroyo Terrace

This house has lost much of its Craftsman look due to the replacement of the shingle exterior with painted stucco.

7 Charles Sumner Greene House (1901–16)
MAP E1 ■ 368 Arroyo Terrace

Charles experimented with many Craftsman ideas while building his own home. The front room, buttressed by boulders and bricks, was a later addition.

8 Duncan-Irwin House (1906)
MAP E1 ■ 240 N Grand Ave

This large, beautiful home, originally a single-story bungalow, pays homage to Japanese design with its slightly upturned roofs.

9 James Culbertson House (1902–15)
MAP E1 ■ 235 N Grand Ave

The stained-glass entrance door, the clinker brick wall, and the pergola are the only original elements of this extensively remodeled home.

10 Halsted House (1905)
MAP E1 ■ 90 N Grand Ave

Originally one of the brothers' smallest designs, this bungalow sports a deep overhang of eaves sheltering the main entrance.

See map on pp90–91 ←

Shopping in Old Pasadena

1 Urban Outfitters
MAP E1 ■ 139 W Colorado Blvd
■ 626-449-1818

Hip, urban clothing, vintage outfits, well-known brands, shoes, gifts, and housewares all under one roof.

Urban Outfitters store

2 Cigars by Chivas
MAP E1 ■ 58 S De Lacey Ave
■ 626-395-7475

This store features a walk-in humidor stocked with cigars from all over the world, plus a cushy lounge area in which you can enjoy them.

3 Restoration Hardware
MAP E1 ■ 127 W Colorado Blvd
■ 626-795-7234

This retro emporium specializes in classic furniture and period hardware, but also has a fun selection of trendy home accessories.

4 Lather
MAP E1 ■ 40 W Colorado Blvd
■ 626-396-9636

This "modern apothecary" uses only natural ingredients for its skincare products and has an assortment of olive oil soap sold by weight.

5 Vroman's Bookstore
MAP E1 ■ 695 E Colorado Blvd
■ 626-449-5320

Vroman's has been going strong since 1894, with knowledgeable and helpful staff, author signings, book readings, and an in-house café.

6 Everson Royce
MAP E1 ■ 155 N Raymond Ave
■ 626-765-9334

A good selection of beer, spirits, and wine – with a range of organic, biodynamic, and natural brands. The shop offers free delivery locally.

7 J. Crew
MAP E1 ■ 46 W Colorado Blvd
■ 626-654-1018

The retail store of this famous catalog line has the same stylish clothing and accessories for men and women at reasonable prices.

8 Homage
MAP E1 ■ 100 N Fair Oaks Ave
■ 626-440-7244

From jewelry to small art pieces, cards, unusual gifts and home decor, this shop features local artisans and has rave-worthy gift wrapping paper.

9 Old Pasadena Pharmacy
MAP E1 ■ 155 S De Lacey Ave
■ 626-844-5000

This beloved store has a full service pharmacy and an eclectic selection of gifts, from hard-to-find beauty brands to cards, accessories, and beer.

10 Gold Bug
MAP E1 ■ 38 E Holly St
■ 626-744-9963

This unusual boutique stocks a huge assortment of organic jewelry, artworks, home-decor pieces, and nature-based oddities.

Unique artworks at Gold Bug

Places to Eat

PRICE CATEGORIES
Price categories include a three-course meal for one, a glass of house wine, and all unavoidable extra charges including tax.

$ under $30 $$ $30–$60 $$$ $60–$90
$$$$ over $90

1 Saladang Garden
MAP E2 ■ 383 S Fair Oaks Ave
■ 626-793-5200 ■ $$

Complex flavors and a lovely Post-Modern patio make this trendy Thai restaurant a Pasadena favorite.

2 Union Restaurant
MAP E1 ■ 37 E Union St
■ 626-795-5841 ■ $$$

Northern Italy meets California at this intimate neighborhood restaurant. The small plates – designed for sharing – are made from locally sourced ingredients.

3 Marston's
MAP E1 ■ 151 E Walnut St
■ 626-796-2459 ■ $

Start the day with blueberry pancakes, golden French toast, or other breakfast favorites at this cottage hangout.

4 The Raymond
MAP E2 ■ 1250 S Fair Oaks Ave at Columbia St ■ 626-441-3136 ■ Closed Mon ■ $$$

This Craftsman-style cottage has a menu of American classics, with plenty of options for vegetarians.

5 Parkway Grill
MAP E1 ■ 510 S Arroyo Parkway ■ 626-795-1001 ■ $$$

Only the freshest organic ingredients are used to perfect Parkway Grill's inspired Californian cuisine.

6 La Grande Orange Cafe
MAP E1 ■ 260 S Raymond Ave
■ 626-356-4444 ■ $$

Housed in the restored Del Mar train station (the Metro rail stops right outside), this family-friendly restaurant offers a well-prepared, standard American and Californian-Mexican

La Grande Orange Cafe dining area

menu with an upscale twist. The charming outdoor patio seating area is the perfect spot for brunch.

7 Bistro 45
MAP E1 ■ 45 S Mentor Ave
■ 626-795-2478 ■ Closed Mon ■ $$$

This classy place in an Art Deco building turns out excellent French fare paired with one of the best wine lists in town. The menu has limited options for vegetarians.

8 Café Santorini
MAP E1 ■ 64 W Union St
■ 626-564-4200 ■ $$

The tables on the terrace are the most coveted on balmy summer evenings. The Greek and Italian menu has lots of fun appetizers.

9 Sushi Roku
MAP E1 ■ 33 Miller Alley
■ 626-683-3000 ■ $$$

Classic sushi and creative new takes on Asian food keep this attractively designed place busy.

10 Zankou Chicken
MAP E1 ■ 1296 E Colorado Blvd
■ 626-405-1502 ■ $

Armenian-owned restaurant specializing in *tarna* (chicken with hummus, salad, and garlic sauce), and *shawarma* kebabs.

See map on pp90–91 ←

🔟 Hollywood

The Hollywood Walk of Fame

Hollywood is at once a town, an industry, and an illusion, and you'll experience all of these along the famed Hollywood Boulevard. Its history encompasses the birth of the movies, the Golden Age of film, and a crushing decline as the studios moved elsewhere. Hollywood has since seen a renaissance along the boulevard – the Ovation Hollywood complex was a major development, and many of the grand movie palaces now once again host film openings. At its core, Hollywood is a museum – the huge sign in the hills, the Walk of Fame, the bars that hosted greats such as Ernest Hemingway – this is still the place to rekindle childhood dreams about the "stars".

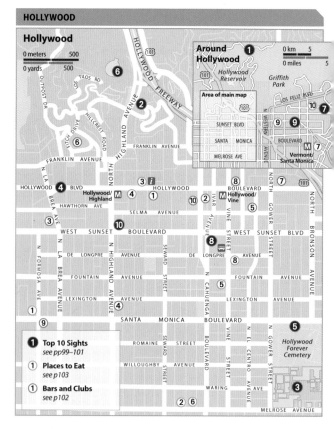

HOLLYWOOD

Hollywood

1	**Top 10 Sights** see pp99–101
1	**Places to Eat** see p103
1	**Bars and Clubs** see p102

1 Hollywood Sign
MAP D2 ■ www.
hollywoodsign.org

From the very beginning, the shiny white Hollywood Sign atop Mount Lee was meant to attract attention, originally for the real estate developer and publisher Harry Chandler. Built in 1923 at a cost of $21,000, the sign was once illuminated by 4,000 bulbs and had its own caretaker. Each letter is 50-ft (15-m) tall and is made of sheet metal. It was rebuilt in 1978 at a cost of more than $250,000. For a more detailed history of the sign and hiking trails that get you close to it, visit the website.

2 Hollywood Heritage Museum
MAP P1 ■ 2100 N Highland Ave
■ 323-874-2276 ■ Open 11am–3pm
Fri–Sun ■ Adm

This museum is housed in the barn where Jesse Lasky and Cecil B. DeMille set up Hollywood's first major film studio in 1913. It was originally located at Selma Avenue and Vine Street, and DeMille shot the first full-length feature *The Squaw Man* here in 1913–14. Exhibits include a re-created studio, photographs, props, and memorabilia from the silent movie era.

3 Paramount Studios
MAP R4 ■ 5555 Melrose Ave
■ 323-956-1777 (reservations
required) ■ Adm

The only major movie studio still located in Hollywood, Paramount began making movies with the Paramount logo in 1916. The studio has always turned out classics and, in 1929 its feature *Wings* took home the first ever Best Picture Oscar. Its most successful movies include *Psycho*, *The Godfather*, *Forrest Gump*, and *Titanic*. Two-hour tours of the studio run daily.

Paramount Studios entrance

4 Hollywood Boulevard
MAP P2

Hollywood's main artery (see pp12–13), one of the district's most glamorous streets during its pre-World War II heyday, was revitalized a few decades ago. The rejuvenation project has focussed on the Ovation Hollywood complex, but old favorites such as TCL Chinese Theatre (see p63) and the Walk of Fame have also received a fresh sheen.

Hollywood Boulevard at dusk

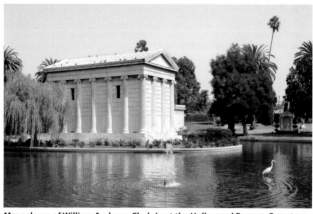
Mausoleum of William Andrews Clark Jr. at the Hollywood Forever Cemetery

5 Hollywood Forever Cemetery

MAP R3 ▪ 6000 Santa Monica Blvd ▪ 323-469-1181 ▪ Open seasonal hours ▪ www.hollywoodforever.com

Founded in 1899, this cemetery is where the famous are buried. The list of those interred here includes Rudolph Valentino, Jane Mansfield, and Cecil B. DeMille. The grandest memorial belongs to Douglas Fairbanks Sr. who, since 2000, has shared his marble tomb with his son, Douglas Jr. A map is available from the nearby flower shop.

Concert at the Hollywood Bowl

6 Hollywood Bowl

MAP P1 ▪ 2301 N Highland Ave ▪ 323-850-2000 ▪ Concerts Tue–Sun late Jun–mid-Sep (tickets required) ▪ www.hollywoodbowl.com

A night at the world's largest natural amphitheater is as much part of Los Angeles summer tradition as backyard barbecues and fun at the beach. The world's finest artists – from Sinatra to Pavarotti – have performed here since 1922. In 1924, Frank Lloyd Wright designed the first concert shell, improving acoustics.

7 Los Feliz and Silver Lake

MAP D2 ▪ Ennis House, 2655 Glendower Ave, closed to the public ▪ Lovell House, 4616 Dundee Dr, closed to the public ▪ Take B Line to Loz Feliz (Vermont Station)

The twin neighborhoods of Los Feliz and Silver Lake, with their alternative, chic dining, shopping, and nightlife, constitute one of Los Angeles's oldest movie colonies. The hills are studded with architectural Modernist masterpieces such as Lloyd Wright's 1924 Ennis House and the Lovell House built by Richard Neutra.

HOLLYWOOD SIGN

Over time the Hollywood Sign lost not only its last four letters (it was originally "Hollywoodland") but also its luster, along with the rest of Hollywood. A "save-the-sign" campaign in 1978 received the help of celebrities such as Alice Cooper, who bought the second O in honor of Groucho Marx. The sign is celebrating its 100th anniversary in 2023.

⑧ Cinerama Dome
MAP Q3

A Hollywood landmark, this white dome of interlocked triangles is LA's most unusual movie theater. The concrete geodesic dome was built by Welton Beckett in 1963 to show Cinerama movies, a wide-screen technique requiring three 35 mm projectors. The ArcLight theaters *(see p62)* are undergoing renovations and will reopen in 2024.

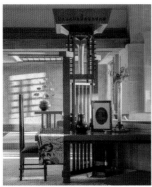

The interior of Hollyhock House

⑨ Hollyhock House
MAP D2 ▪ 4800 Hollywood Blvd ▪ 323-644-6269 ▪ Tours: hours vary, call ahead ▪ **Adm** (free for under 13s)

The Mayan-style mansion, designed by Lloyd Wright in 1921 for oil heiress Aline Barnsdall, anchors a community arts center. Depictions of the hollyhock, her favorite flower, appear everywhere on facades and furniture.

⑩ Crossroads of the World
MAP P3 ▪ 6671 Sunset Blvd

The centerpiece of this unique architectural metaphor is a ship-like Art Deco building that "sails" into a courtyard flanked by cottages in styles ranging from Spanish Colonial to German gingerbread. A quiet office complex, it was built in 1936 by Robert Derrah, who designed the Coca-Cola Bottling Plant *(see p81)*.

A DAY WITH THE STARS

▶ MORNING

Begin at La Brea Avenue and Hollywood Boulevard, heading east to the **Hollywood Roosevelt Hotel** *(see p12)*, home of the first Academy Awards. In the **TCL Chinese Theatre** *(see p63)* you can stand on the footprints of your favorite stars. An escalator will whisk you into the vast **Ovation Hollywood** complex *(see p13)* with great shopping and views of the **Hollywood Sign** *(see p99)* and the dazzling **El Capitan** *(see p63)*. Stop by the **Hollywood Museum** *(1660 N Highland)* to see props, costumes, and sets from film favorites before taking a two-block detour south on Highland Avenue to **Hollywood High School** *(1521 N Highland)*, alma mater of Lawrence Fishburne. Have your picture taken with the stars (almost) at **Madame Tussauds Hollywood** *(7024 Hollywood Blvd)*. From there, head east for a delicious lunch at **Rao's Hollywood** *(see p103)*.

AFTERNOON

Back on Hollywood Boulevard, you'll come across the **Egyptian Theatre** *(see p62)* and, at No. 6667, **Musso & Frank Grill** *(see p103)*, the oldest restaurant in Hollywood, once the haunt of Chaplin, Hemingway, and other famous people. Wrap up the day with drinks and sunset views at **Yamashiro Restaurant** *(see p102)*, followed by a burger and a Guinness milkshake at the popular and trendy **25 Degrees** at the Hollywood Roosevelt Hotel *(7000 Hollywood Blvd)*.

See map on p98 ←

Bars and Clubs

The dimly lit Art Deco-style bar at Boardner's, built in 1942

1 Boardner's
MAP P2 ■ 1652 N Cherokee Ave ■ 323-462-9621 ■ www.boardners.com
This historical bar has a large dance floor and live entertainment.

2 The Room Hollywood
MAP Q2 ■ 1626 N Cahuenga Blvd ■ 866-687-4499 ■ www.theroomhollywood.com
Dance to hip hop, R&B, and occasional old rock at this stylish club.

3 The Woods
MAP P2 ■ 1533 N La Brea Ave ■ 323-876-6612 ■ www.vintagebargroup.com
Hidden in a nondescript mini-mall, this quaint lounge features live bands.

4 Next Door Lounge
MAP P2 ■ 1154 N Highland ■ 213-693-1530 ■ www.nextdoorhollywood.com
A dance floor, live entertainment, a fast cocktail service, and weekend shows make for a lively night out.

5 Good Times at Davey Wayne's
MAP Q2 ■ 1611 N El Centro Ave ■ 323-498-0859 ■ www.goodtimesatdaveywaynes.com
Creative cocktails and alcohol-infused snow cones are served at this retro bar.

6 Yamashiro Restaurant
MAP P2 ■ 1999 N Sycamore Ave ■ 323-466-5125 ■ www.yamashirorestaurant.com
A spot for sunset drinks and Japanese food with gorgeous city views.

7 Academy LA
MAP Q2 ■ 6021 Hollywood Blvd ■ 323-785-2680 ■ www.academy.la
Top DJs and live electronic music attract large crowds. Tickets sell out early, so call ahead.

8 Frolic Room
MAP Q2 ■ 6245 Hollywood Blvd ■ 323-462-5890 ■ www.frolicroomla.com
Bartenders wearing bow ties and vests pour the drinks here, while the jukebox entertains.

9 Formosa Café
MAP P3 ■ 7156 Santa Monica Blvd ■ 323-850-1014 ■ www.theformosacafe.com
Where Humphrey Bogart and Marilyn Monroe once hung out. Enjoy the Mai Tais and tasty California-Asian treats.

10 Burgundy Room
MAP P2 ■ 1621 1/2 N Cahuenga Blvd ■ 323-465-7530
A dive bar with an eclectic mix of music, from country western to punk. Good for pre- or post-dinner drinks.

Places to Eat

① Jones Hollywood
MAP N3 ■ 7205 Santa Monica Blvd ■ 323-850-1726 ■ Closed lunch ■ $$$

Popular with the locals, this little spot serves classic thin-crust pizza, spaghetti and meatballs, and for many, the best apple pie in town.

② Marino
MAP Q4 ■ 6001 Melrose Ave ■ 323-466-8812 ■ $$$$

Classic New York Italian-style dishes and a lengthy wine list make this 50-year-old place a local favorite.

③ Musso & Frank Grill
MAP P2 ■ 6667 Hollywood Blvd ■ 323-467-7788 ■ $$$

Steaks and chops dominate the menu of Hollywood's oldest restaurant (open since 1919). It was a major hangout for celebrities such as Hemingway.

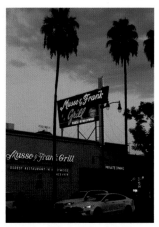

Entrance of Musso & Frank Grill

④ Rao's Hollywood
MAP Q3 ■ 1006 Seward St ■ 323-962-7267 ■ $$$$

This branch of the Harlem original earns consistently high marks for its homestyle Italian fare and wine. It has a cozy dining room and the service is excellent.

PRICE CATEGORIES
Price categories include a three-course meal for one, a glass of house wine, and all unavoidable extra charges including tax.

$ under $30 $$ $30–$60 $$$ $60–$90 $$$$ over $90

---

⑤ La Numero Uno
MAP Q2 ■ 1247 Vine St ■ 323-957-1111 ■ $

A good place for Mexican and Salvadoran specialties such as tamales, pupusas, enchiladas with sides of fried plantains and yucca root.

⑥ Providence
MAP Q4 ■ 5955 Melrose Ave ■ 323-460-4170 ■ $$$$

Fresh seafood, tasting menus and an extensive wine list are the draw at this elegant, romantic spot (see p66).

⑦ Café Stella
MAP D2 ■ 3932 W Sunset Blvd ■ 323-666-0265 ■ Closed Sun & Mon ■ $$

This romantic French-style bistro offers mostly outdoor seating in a lovely courtyard with hanging amber lights and olive and lavender plants.

⑧ Los Balcones del Peru
MAP Q3 ■ 1360 Vine St ■ 323-871-9600 ■ $$

This is a casual spot for delicious Peruvian food. Wash it all down with Argentinian wine or Peruvian beer.

⑨ Jitlada Restaurant
MAP D2 ■ 5233 W Sunset Blvd ■ 323-667-9809 ■ Closed Mon ■ $$

Considered by many to be the best Thai restaurant in LA, Jitlada serves delicious curries and papaya salads.

⑩ Yuca's Hut
MAP D2 ■ 2056 Hillhurst Ave, Los Feliz ■ 323-662-1214 ■ Closed Sun ■ No credit cards ■ $

Head this way for yummy Mexican food. Try the *cochinita pibil* tacos. Only non-vegetarian food is served here.

See map on p98 ←

🔟 West Hollywood and Midtown

West Hollywood is LA's party zone and teems with nightclubs, restaurants, bars, and comedy clubs. After dark, Sunset Strip is the center of the action for film producers and fashionable locals. This is also LA's LGBTQ+ quarter, especially along Santa Monica Boulevard. For shopaholics there's Melrose Avenue, a quirky pathway lined with designer stores, tattoo parlors, Gothic-chic shops, and bustling cafés and delis. It's also home to the Pacific Design Center, the anchor of the West Hollywood Design District. For cultural edification, head south to an amorphous district we've termed "Midtown," whose main artery, Wilshire Boulevard, boasts some of the city's finest museums along the historic Miracle Mile.

Historic trolley on The Grove

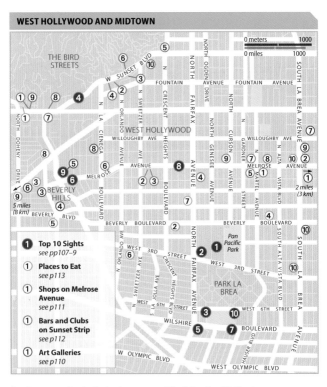

WEST HOLLYWOOD AND MIDTOWN

① **Top 10 Sights**
see pp107–9

① **Places to Eat**
see p113

① **Shops on Melrose Avenue**
see p111

① **Bars and Clubs on Sunset Strip**
see p112

① **Art Galleries**
see p110

Previous pages Resplendent arches, campus of the University of California

1 The Grove

MAP N5 ■ 189 The Grove Dr
■ 323-900-8000 ■ Open 10am–9pm
Mon–Thu, 10am–10pm Fri & Sat,
10am–8pm Sun

Adjoining the Original Farmers Market, the Grove is an upscale outdoor shopping and dining center with a 14-screen movie theater. This mall features highlights such as a historic trolley and a fountain with a water show set to music. Along with adjacent CBS Television City and the Farmers Market, the Grove occupies land once owned by the Gilmore family. Gilmore Stadium, home of the Hollywood Stars, a baseball team owned by Bing Crosby, Cecil B. DeMille, and Barbara Stanwyck, was once located where CBS now stands.

2 Original Farmers Market

MAP M5 ■ 6333 W 3rd St
■ 323-933-9211 ■ Open 9am–9pm
Mon–Fri, 10am–9pm Sat, 10am–7pm
Sun ■ www.farmersmarketla.com

In 1934, two entrepreneurs asked landowner E. B. Gilmore for permission to start a produce market on a vacant parking lot on his property. Soon after, a group of farmers started selling fresh fruit, flowers, and vegetables from trucks. Many of the 150 stalls of the Farmers Market, such as Magee's House of Nuts, have been in the same families for generations. Scouts from nearby CBS TV City roam in search of game-show audience members.

Twelve Months of the Year, **LACMA**

3 Los Angeles County Museum of Art (LACMA)

LACMA *(see pp20–23)* has one of the finest collections of art in the US. The museum's renovation, scheduled to be completed in 2024, will enable important works from its extensive permanent collection to be on display alongside rotating exhibitions.

4 Sunset Strip

Sunset Strip has been LA's nocturnal hub since the 1920s and is the most history-laden section of the 25-mile (40-km) Sunset Boulevard. Several developments have brought a high-end sheen to this formerly neglected stretch, with new hotels and clubs attracting visitors. The iconic Chateau Marmont, the Whisky a Go-Go, the Mondrian Hotel with its exclusive SkyBar, and the Viper Room *(see pp14–15)*, still attract stars and fans.

Farmers Market

Futuristic building of the Petersen Automotive Museum

5 Petersen Automotive Museum

MAP M6 ■ 6060 Wilshire Blvd, Miracle Mile ■ 323-964-6331 ■ Open 10am–5pm daily ■ Adm

LA's evolution from sleepy outpost to sweeping megalopolis is uniquely tied to the rise of the automobile. This is the basic premise of this wonderful museum, which does a lot more than display pretty vintage cars (though there are plenty of those, too). The museum's exterior is hard to miss from afar. Refreshed in 2015, the museum's facade features rolling steel ribbons representing a car zooming past the iconic corner. Inside, the cars take center stage. Exhibits change regularly, but they usually include galleries devoted to hot rods, motorcycles, and vehicles owned by celebrities or used in movies. For children, the Discovery Center makes science fun.

6 West Hollywood Design District

MAP L4 ■ Along Beverly Blvd, Robertson Blvd, & Melrose Ave between La Cienega Blvd & Doheny Dr

The streets surrounding the Pacific Design Center (PDC) are flanked with design stores where you can actually buy – and not just look at (as in the PDC) – what you see. Best explored on foot, the district is filled with cutting-edge art galleries (see p110), trendy restaurants, and cafés.

7 Craft Contemporary

MAP N6 ■ 5814 Wilshire Blvd, Miracle Mile ■ 323-937-4230 ■ Open 11am–5pm Tue–Sun ■ Adm (free for under 10s; free Sun) ■ www.cafam.org

This small museum is dedicated to showcasing handicrafts and folk art from around the world. The brainchild of folk art collector Edith Wyle, it was originally launched in 1965 as "The Egg and The Eye," a gallery space and omelet restaurant. Apart from its changing exhibits, the museum is best known for its family-friendly mask making nights, open craft labs, and workshops.

8 Melrose Avenue

Decorated with vibrant street art, Melrose Avenue (see p111) is still a haven for Hollywood hipsters and the place to stock up on vintage threads, provocative fashions, and unusual gift items. Weekend afternoons are prime time for soaking it all up.

Fashion from Melrose Avenue

LGBTQ+ LOS ANGELES

West Hollywood is the center of LA's LGBTQ+ community. There's plenty of partying in the many happening bars, clubs, cafés, and restaurants along Santa Monica Boulevard. Huge crowds turn up for the colorful LA Pride Parade and Festival in June and the wonderfully outrageous Halloween Carnival.

9 Pacific Design Center (PDC)

MAP L4 ■ 8687 Melrose Ave ■ 310-657-0800, 310-360-6418 (showrooms) ■ Open 9am–5pm Mon–Fri ■ www.pacificdesigncenter.com

More than 100 showrooms in this complex display the finest in furniture, fabrics, lighting, and accessories. With a contemporary 1975 design by Cesar Pelli the most striking feature of the PDC is the blue glass facade, known as "The Blue Whale." For ongoing public events at PDC, check the website. Currently there are two restaurants, Silver Bullet Express and Pacific Design Café, which are open to the public. Visitors who wish to see the showrooms can call for admission ahead of time.

Page Museum entrance

10 La Brea Tar Pits and Museum

MAP N6 ■ 5801 Wilshire Blvd, Miracle Mile ■ 323-934-7243 ■ Open 9:30am–5:30pm Wed–Mon ■ Adm ■ www.tarpits.org

Mammoths, saber-toothed cats, and dire wolves are the stars here, offering a look at life in LA during the last Ice Age. Since 1906, excavations at the pits adjacent to the museum have yielded over a million fossilized bones of about 450 species of insects, birds, and mammals, which are now on display. There is also a glass-walled laboratory where paleontologists may be seen working. Outside the museum, life-size replicas of mammoths trapped in muck dramatize the ghastly fate of Los Angeles's prehistoric denizens. Visitors should note that there is a $18 parking fee.

A DAY IN HOLLYWOOD

▶ **MORNING**

Start your day at Wilshire Boulevard's "Museum Row" to catch the latest headline exhibit at **LACMA** (see pp20–23) and to see selections from its superb permanent collection. If you can muster the energy before lunch, head to the **Petersen Automotive Museum** or the **Page Museum**.

After leaving Museum Row, drive a few blocks north to **The Original Farmers Market** (see p107), and try the Cajun food at Gumbo Pot, or the all-American menu at Du-Par's.

AFTERNOON

For an afternoon of shopping, start with the Farmers Market itself, then wander over to **The Grove** (see p107), an outdoor mall. Head north on Fairfax Avenue, turning right on **Melrose Avenue**. This quintessential LA shopping street is packed with fun and funky stores and offers great people-watching opportunities, especially on weekends.

Head off for an early dinner at **Canter's Deli** (see p113), with its famous mile-high Jewish deli sandwiches, then drive up to **Sunset Strip** (see p107) for an evening of laughs at the **Comedy Store** (see p65) or **The Laugh Factory** (see p65). Make your reservations in advance. Showtime is usually 8pm. Round off your day with a drink at **SkyBar** (see p112) or the lounge at the chic **Harriet's Rooftop** (see p146).

See map on p106 ←

Art Galleries

1 Morán Morán
MAP L4 ▪ 641 N Western Ave
▪ 800-535-9850

A spacious gallery exhibiting trendsetting contemporary work by several artists.

2 Hauser & Wirth
MAP X5 ▪ 8980 Santa Monica Blvd ▪ 424-404-1200

For its second LA location, this posh New York gallery turned a vintage car showroom into 6,000 ft (1,829 m) of exhibition space where international artists are featured.

3 George Stern Fine Arts
MAP K4 ▪ 501 N Robertson ▪ 310-276-2600

This gallery specializes in late 19th- and early 20th-century Impressionist landscape painters based in California such as Guy Rose.

4 Leica Store and Gallery
MAP L5 ▪ 8783 Beverly Blvd ▪ 424-777-0341

In addition to a sales showroom of Leica cameras, a gallery celebrates the world through the lenses of the world's finest photographers.

5 Hamilton-Selway Fine Art Gallery
MAP L4 ▪ 8678 Melrose Ave ▪ 310-657-1711

Home to the largest collection of Andy Warhol originals on the West Coast, this gallery also features Roy Lichtenstein, Keith Haring, and other pop art icons.

6 Louis Stern Fine Arts
MAP M4 ▪ 9002 Melrose Ave ▪ 310-276-0147

Mid-century abstract artists from the West Coast are featured in this gallery. It also acts as an agent for private parties selling impressionist, modern and Latin American art.

7 Jeffrey Deitch Gallery
MAP P4 ▪ 925 N Orange Dr ▪ 323-925-3000

Known for its innovative exhibitions that push multimedia boundaries, this contemporary gallery is owned by curator and dealer Jeffrey Deitch.

8 Gallery 825
MAP L3 ▪ 825 La Cienega Blvd ▪ 310-652-8272

Owned by the Los Angeles Art Association, it has four exhibit areas showing works by its cooperative members. All genres are represented, with a focus on contemporary art.

9 Various Small Fires
MAP P4 ▪ 812 N Highland Ave ▪ 310-426-8040

With multiple locations in Dallas and Seoul, this gallery displays works that focus on social, political, and environmental issues.

10 Fahey/Klein Gallery
MAP P5 ▪ 148 N La Brea Ave ▪ 323-934-2250

A power in the world of rare, vintage, and contemporary art photography, Fahey/Klein showcases Henri Cartier-Bresson and other artists.

Fine art photography exhibition at Fahey/Klein Gallery

Shops on Melrose Avenue

Jewelry galore at Maya Jewelry

⑥ l.a.Eyeworks
MAP N4 ▪ 7407 Melrose Ave
▪ 323-653-8255

This unusual and vibrant store is known for featuring the most unique eyeglass designs on the planet and attracts its share of the hip crowd.

⑧ Mega City One
MAP N4 ▪ 7301 Melrose Ave
▪ 323-934-3373

A packed store offering a great selection of comic books, graphic novels, board games, and collectibles.

① Maya Jewelry
MAP N4 ▪ 7360 Melrose Ave
▪ 323-655-2708

This small store stocks affordable jewelry, mostly made out of silver. It also has a great mask collection.

⑧ Flasher
MAP N4 ▪ 7609 Melrose Ave
▪ 323-655-3375

A uniquely eclectic store that specializes in flashy statement pieces for people looking to stand out, or those who want to add an artistic, urban edge to their wardrobes.

② Decades
MAP M4 ▪ 8214 Melrose Ave
▪ 323-655-1960

If Rodeo Drive is out of your league, try this couture resale boutique that stocks second-hand clothing and 1960s and 1970s Pucci and Courrèges.

③ Reformation
MAP M4 ▪ 8000 Melrose Ave
▪ 213-408-4154

With high prices but simple silhouettes, LA's hip, eco-friendly dresswear experts, Reformation, offer top sustainable styles for your wardrobe.

⑨ Joyrich
MAP P5 ▪ 7700 Melrose Ave
▪ 323-944-0631

Joyrich founder Tim Hirota is the creative genius behind some of LA's latest premium streetwear trends. His Melrose flagship store showcases the latest designs and styles.

⑩ Melrose Trading Post
MAP M4 ▪ At the corner of Melrose & Fairfax Aves ▪ 323-655-7679

This cool Sunday flea market offers vintage fashions, collectibles, and retro furnishings.

④ Wasteland
MAP N4 ▪ 7428 Melrose Ave
▪ 323-653-3028

Stylists and bargain-hunters shop for vintage clothing, accessories, and shoes at this warehouse-sized store.

⑤ Wanna Buy a Watch?
MAP N4 ▪ 8411 Melrose Ave
▪ 323-653-0467

This classy store is known for its fine selection of vintage and contemporary watches, antique diamond rings, and 1920s Art Nouveau baubles.

Stalls at the Melrose Trading Post

See map on p106 ←

Bars and Clubs on Sunset Strip

1 Rainbow Bar & Grill
MAP K3 ■ 9015 Sunset Blvd
■ 310-278-4232

Rock'n'roll devotees flock to this legendary bar filled with photos, records, and guitars of every headliner rocker group imaginable.

Upscale SkyBar, with its famous pool

2 SkyBar
MAP M3 ■ 8440 Sunset Blvd, at the Mondrian Hotel
■ 323-848-6025

Famous for its poolside cocktails, celebrity crowd, and sweeping city views. Getting past the velvet rope here is a tall order.

3 The Tower Bar
MAP M3 ■ 8358 Sunset Blvd
■ 323-848-6677

This upscale, walnut-paneled lounge has just the right Old Hollywood feel. Enjoy good cocktails, poolside dining, and spectacular views.

4 Harriet's Rooftop
MAP L3 ■ 8490 Sunset Blvd
■ 424-281-1860

Located on the roof of 1 Hotel, this classy green pin-striped lounge has open-air verandahs and offers great views across West Hollywood.

5 Hyde Sunset Kitchen & Cocktails
MAP M3 ■ 8117 Sunset Blvd
■ 323-716-4200

Expect exclusivity and attitude at this celeb-heavy nightclub, with private tables and large couches.

6 Saddle Ranch Chop House
MAP M3 ■ 8371 W Sunset Blvd
■ 323-656-2007

A Texas-style steakhouse popular with families until 10pm, when it becomes a lively night-time hangout.

7 The Viper Room
MAP L3 ■ 8852 Sunset Blvd
■ 310-358-1881

Local musicians stage concerts at this famous club, which once saw Bruce Springsteen perform. *(see p15)*.

8 Whisky a Go-Go
MAP L3 ■ 8901 W Sunset Blvd
■ 310-652-4202

LA's epicenter of rock'n'roll in the 1960s, this club found fame for The Doors and still books new bands.

9 The Roxy
MAP K3 ■ 9009 W Sunset Blvd
■ 310-278-9457

This no-nonsense club is loved by serious fans as its focus is on the show, not the decor or the crowd.

Colorful entrance to The Roxy

10 The Den on Sunset
MAP M3 ■ 8226 Sunset Blvd
■ 323-656-0336

Keen to be part of the Strip's recent glow up from rock and roll to glamourous swank, The Den transformed its low-key red booths to an inviting modern lounge. Reservations are recommended and no cash is accepted.

See map on p106

Places to Eat

(1) Night+Market WeHo
MAP K4 ■ 9043 Sunset Blvd
■ 310-275-9724 ■ $$

This casual restaurant offers Thai street food, ice cream sandwiches, beer and an extensive wine list. The Fried Chicken Sandwich is a must try.

(2) Swingers
MAP M5 ■ 8020 Beverly Blvd
■ 323-653-5858 ■ $$

This retro diner with its plaid booths and Andy Warhol wallpaper serves steamy chicken soup and bulging sandwiches until the wee hours.

(3) Gracias Madre
MAP L4 ■ 8905 Melrose Ave
■ 323-978-2170 ■ $$

This airy vegan haven serves tasty Mexican food and refreshing cocktails on a giant open-air patio.

(4) Angelini Osteria
MAP N5 ■ 7313 Beverly Blvd
■ 323-297-0070 ■ Veg: On request
■ $$$

Having cooked for the Pope and presidents, Chef Angelini now delights foodies with his comfort food.

(5) The Ivy
MAP L4 ■ 113 N Robertson Blvd ■ 310-274-8303 ■ $$$$

Join the stars in two dining rooms filled with flowers. Try the Caesar salad or the crispy crab cakes.

Floral decorations at The Ivy

PRICE CATEGORIES
Price categories include a three-course meal for one, a glass of house wine, and all unavoidable extra charges including tax.

$ under $30 $$ $30–$60 $$$ $60–$90
$$$$ over $90

---

(6) Joan's on Third
MAP M5 ■ 8350 W 3rd St
■ 323-655-2285 ■ $

This little deli is perfect for gourmets on the go or out for a casual lunch. The tarragon chicken salad is great.

(7) Canter's Deli
MAP M4 ■ 419 N Fairfax
■ 323-651-2030 ■ $$

An LA classic since 1931, this family-owned Jewish-style deli is a popular after-hours spot.

(8) Guisados
MAP L4 ■ 8935 Santa Monica Blvd ■ 310-777-0310 ■ $

A variety of tasty meats topped on corn tortillas are served here.

(9) Echigo
MAP R3 ■ 12217 Santa Monica Blvd ■ 310-820-9787 ■ Closed Sun
■ $$$

Sushi of all types and stripes is on offer, and all of it is fresh.

(10) M Café
MAP P4 ■ 7119 Melrose Ave
■ 323-525-0588 ■ $$

M Café's macrobiotic cuisine has a huge following. Try the exquisite club sandwich with tempeh "bacon."

🔟 Beverly Hills, Westwood, and Bel-Air

With its high-end shopping, elegant restaurants, lush mini-parks, and some of the state's most expensive estates, Beverly Hills embodies Hollywood wealth and glamour. Adjacent Westwood is home to UCLA, one of the finest universities in the country. Bel Air is almost exclusively a residential enclave of mansions. The nearby Getty Center serenely lords above it all in its white majesty.

The iconic Beverly Hills Hotel

1 Beverly Hills Hotel

MAP J4 ■ 9641 Sunset Blvd ■ 310-276-2251 ■ www.beverlyhills hotel.com

LA's most famous hotel *(see p146)* has been part of Hollywood history since its 1912 opening. Douglas Fairbanks Sr. and Will Rogers got drunk in the bar, Howard Hughes rented Bungalow 3 for 30 years, and Marilyn Monroe reportedly met both JFK and RFK here. Political leaders, royals, and film stars have all stayed, partied, and cavorted at the legendary Pink Palace.

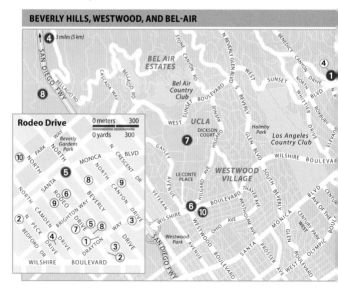

BEVERLY HILLS, WESTWOOD, AND BEL-AIR

Upscale designer boutiques line Rodeo Drive

2 Rodeo Drive

Rodeo Drive *(see p68)* is one of the world's most famous – and expensive – shopping streets, synonymous with a lifestyle of luxury and fame. Only three blocks long, it is essentially a haute couture runway, with all the major international players represented here *(see p118)*. You'll often spot nicely groomed shoppers, although actual star sightings are rare. Rodeo's southern end is punctuated by the Beverly Wilshire *(see p144)*, one of LA's grandest hotels. Architecture fans should check out Frank Lloyd Wright's Anderton Court *(see p118)*.

3 Beverly Hills Civic Center

MAP J5 ▪ East of Crescent Dr between Santa Monica Blvd & Burton Dr

The wealth of a city is often reflected in its public buildings, so it should come as no surprise that Beverly Hills' civic center is the envy of other towns. The elegant City Hall was built in 1932 in Spanish Renaissance style and harmoniously incorporated into a contemporary Spanish-style complex with palm-lined walkways and curved colonnades. It houses a beautiful library.

4 Skirball Cultural Center

MAP C2 ▪ 2701 N Sepulveda Blvd, Brentwood/Bel-Air ▪ 310-440-4500 ▪ Open noon–5pm Tue–Fri, 10am–5pm Sat & Sun ▪ Adm (free for under 2s, free Thu) ▪ www.skir ball.org

This modern Jewish cultural center was named after benefactor Jack Skirball (1896–1985), a rabbi and producer of Hitchcock films. The complex hosts live events and has a multimedia museum. Exhibits explore the parallels between the Jewish experience and the principles of American democracy. The ongoing exhibition, *Visions and Values*, looks at Jewish life from Antiquity to America.

see Rodeo Drive map, right

SUNSET BLVD
FOOTHILL RD
ELEVADO AVE
DRIVE
N RODEO DR
WEST 3RD ST
BURTON WAY
WILSHIRE BOULEVARD
S BEVERLY DRIVE
ROXBURY DRIVE
CHARLEVILLE BLVD
GREGORY
S ROBERTSON BLVD
DOHENY WAY
GREGORY WAY
WEST OLYMPIC BOULEVARD
S BEVERWIL DR
PICO BOULEVARD
CASHIO STREET
Hillcrest Country Club

0 kilometers 1
0 miles 1

5 Wallis Annenberg Center for Performing Arts

MAP K5 ■ 9390 N Santa Monica Blvd ■ 310-746-4000 ■ www.thewallis.org

A modern Beverly Hills institution, this community arts center, known as "The Wallis", is named for philanthropist Wallis Annenberg. The compound opened in 2013 with a foyer built into a restored 1933 Beverly Hills Post Office and a gilded contemporary 500-seat theater designed by LA architect Zoltan Pali. There is a smaller 150-seat theater here as well. A calendar of popular artists and a robust slate of interactive educational events means you can experience anything from chamber orchestras to Latinx ballets to spoken word one-act plays, and more.

Royce Hall entrance, UCLA

6 Hammer Museum

MAP C2 ■ 10899 Wilshire Blvd ■ 310-443-7000 ■ Open 11am–6pm Tue–Sun ■ www.hammer.ucla.edu

This museum, run by UCLA, is the legacy of Armand Hammer, an oil tycoon who discovered a passion for collecting art in the 1920s. Hammer was especially fond of 19th-century French Impressionists such as Monet. Rotating exhibitions are complemented by traveling shows with a more contemporary angle. Free readings, film screenings, and lectures are quite popular. Phone ahead or check the website for the latest events and exhibits.

7 University of California, Los Angeles (UCLA)

MAP C2 ■ 310-825-4321 ■ www.ucla.edu

One of the nation's top research universities, UCLA (founded in 1919) counts many luminaries among its alumni, including Francis Ford Coppola. It has around 150 buildings, with architectural gems such as Royce Hall. The Fowler Museum has a marvellous collection of international art. To the north is the lovely Franklin D. Murphy Sculpture Garden (see p53).

8 The Getty Center

Although best known for its collection of European art, the Getty (see pp16–19) offers much more – a hilltop setting with sweeping views from the ocean to the mountains,

CITY OF CONTRASTS

Out of the nation's largest metro areas, Los Angeles ranks seventh in income inequality. A study infers that this high rate of inequality threatens the region's long-term economic well-being. Both middle-wage and low-wage jobs have declined at a high rate, and the city's neighborhoods are becoming increasingly segregated by race and income.

Exhibition, UCLA Hammer Museum

architecture as exquisite as "frozen music" (to quote Goethe), and landscaped gardens that are nothing less than the finest art.

9 Museum of Tolerance

MAP D2 ▪ 9786 W Pico Blvd ▪ 310-772-2505 ▪ Open 10am–3pm Mon–Thu (until 5pm Sun) ▪ Closed Jewish holidays ▪ Reservations advised ▪ Adm ▪ www.museumoftolerance.com

This high-tech museum, the only museum of its kind in the world, confronts visitors with issues of extreme intolerance to make them realize the need for greater acceptance in today's world. The experience begins at the "Tolerancenter," whose exhibits address issues such as human-rights violations and the Civil Rights movement. The Holocaust section, at the core, chronicles Nazi atrocities. An interesting multimedia exhibit follows the lives of well-known Americans from different ethnic backgrounds.

Marilyn Monroe's epitaph, Westwood

10 Pierce Brothers Westwood Village Memorial Park

MAP C2 ▪ 1218 Glendon Ave ▪ 310-474-1579 ▪ Open 8am–sunset

This small cemetery beneath Westwood's office high-rises has more stars per square yard than any other in LA. Marilyn Monroe's remains rest in an above-ground crypt that is always decorated with flowers (Hugh Hefner was laid to rest in the adjacent spot in 2017). Other celebs buried here are Natalie Wood, Burt Lancaster, and Frank Zappa.

A TOUR OF STARS' HOMES

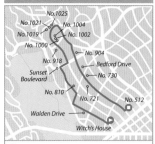

▶ MORNING

Almost every celebrity with ties to Hollywood in the past century has at one time or another lived in these neighborhoods, from Clara Bow in the early days of the "talkies" to Adele, Beyonce, and Jay-Z today. Privacy is paramount, however, so the mansions now are hidden behind high walls and locked gates. Begin your tour of stars' homes by driving north on **Walden Drive**, just off Santa Monica Boulevard, for a glimpse of the "**Witch's House**", located at the corner of Carmelita Avenue and famous for its Hansel-and-Gretel looks. Go right on Lomitas Avenue, then left on Linden Drive, where mobster Bugsy Siegel was shot at **No. 810** in 1947. Follow Linden north to Sunset Boulevard, turn right, then left on Roxbury Drive for two star-packed blocks. As well as Jimmy Stewart's former home at **No. 918**, you'll see the erstwhile homes of song lyricist Ira Gershwin (**No. 1021**), Diane Keaton (**No. 1025**), singer Rosemary Clooney (aunt of George, at **No. 1019**), Peter Falk (**No. 1004**), comedian Jack Benny (**No. 1002**), and Lucille Ball (**No. 1000**).

Turn right on Canyon Drive, then right again on Bedford Drive, where the house at **No. 904** was at different times the home of stars such as Frank Sinatra, Rex Harrison, Anthony Quinn, Greta Garbo and Ava Gardner. Steve Martin used to live at **No. 721** and Lana Turner at **No. 730**. **No. 512** is the former home of silent screen siren Clara Bow.

See map on pp114–15 ←

Temptations on Rodeo Drive

Bijan's branded luxury car parked outside the exclusive boutique

1 Two Rodeo
MAP J6 ▪ Rodeo Dr at Wilshire Blvd

This cobbled lane resembles an idealized European shopping avenue with fountains and a piazza. When it opened in 1990, it was the first new street in Beverly Hills since 1914.

2 Tiffany & Co
MAP J5 ▪ 210 N Rodeo Dr ▪ 310-273-8880

Admire the meticulously crafted jewelry in this luxury store. The branch in New York was famously used as a backdrop in *Breakfast at Tiffany's*.

3 Pomellato
MAP J5 ▪ 214 N Rodeo Dr ▪ 310-550-5639

This Italian luxury jewelry brand is known for its innovative cuts of colored stones set in avant-garde designs of high-karat gold.

4 Louis Vuitton
MAP J5 ▪ 295 N Rodeo Dr ▪ 310-887-2777

Known for its signature leather goods, it also stocks fragrances, fine watches, jewelry, and made-to-order shoes.

5 Anderton Court
MAP J5 ▪ 333 N Rodeo Dr

One of Frank Lloyd Wright's later buildings (1952), the zigzagging ramp around a well of light is reminiscent of New York's Guggenheim Museum.

6 Bijan
MAP J5 ▪ 443 N Rodeo Dr ▪ 310-273-6544 ▪ By appointment only

This boutique stocks quality menswear which is said to be the world's most expensive. Famous client names are etched into the window.

7 Gucci
MAP J5 ▪ 347 N Rodeo Dr ▪ 310-278-3451

The store is a sure-fire winner in the looks department, but most customers have eyes only for the trademark shoes and handbags.

8 Harry Winston
MAP J5 ▪ 310 N Rodeo Dr ▪ 310-271-8554

On Oscar night, when the stars come out in their diamonds, they're most likely on loan from here, one of the world's most exclusive jewelers.

9 The Rodeo Collection
MAP J5 ▪ 421 N Rodeo Dr

A white marble outdoor shopping mall with five floors of boutiques orbiting a sunken atrium courtyard with a fancy restaurant.

10 O'Neill House
MAP J5 ▪ 507 N Rodeo Dr ▪ Closed to the public

This 1988 complex sports whimsical Art Nouveau design elements borrowed from architect Gaudí.

Places to Eat

1 Spago Beverly Hills
MAP K5 ■ 176 N Canon Dr
■ 310-385-0880 ■ $$$$

Stargazers are likely to report sightings when dining at Wolfgang Puck's flagship restaurant *(see p67)*.

2 Crustacean
MAP J5 ■ 9646 S Santa Monica Blvd ■ 310-205-8990 ■ $$$

A Beverly Hills hot spot, Crustacean serves refined Vietnamese cuisine. Try anything made with the owner/chef's "secret spices."

3 The Palm
MAP K5 ■ 267 N Canon Dr
■ 310-550-8811 ■ $$$$

This classic steakhouse is noted for its excellent service and caricatures of the stars that line the walls. Start out with the crab cakes, but save room for the generous deserts.

Courtyard dining at the Polo Lounge

4 Polo Lounge
MAP J4 ■ 9641 Sunset Blvd
■ 310-887-2777 ■ $$$$

This restaurant, located in the Beverly Hills Hotel, mixes signature dishes such as McCarthy salad with Asian and Californian cuisine.

5 Belvedere
MAP J5 ■ 9882 Santa Monica Blvd ■ 310-551-2888 ■ $$$

Hollywood power brokers love the dining room, decorated with artworks,

PRICE CATEGORIES
Price categories include a three-course meal for one, a glass of house wine, and all unavoidable extra charges including tax.

$ under $30 $$ $30–$60 $$$ $60–$90 $$$$ over $90

and impeccable service here. The menu changes with the seasons to make the most of local produce.

6 Maude
MAP ■ 212 S Beverly Dr
■ 310-859-3418 ■ $$$$

A new tasting menu every three months highlights seasonal specialties inspired by the world's leading wine regions. Reservations are a must for this cozy restaurant *(see p67)*.

7 Matsuhisa
MAP L5 ■ 129 N La Cienega Blvd ■ 310-659-9639 ■ $$$

This is the original of Nobu Matsuhisa's small but growing empire of Japanese-Peruvian seafood restaurants. Ignore the menu and surrender to the chef's formidable imagination.

8 Nate'n Al
MAP J5 ■ 414 N Beverly Dr
■ 310-274-0101 ■ $

This modest kosher deli has been catering to the stars since 1943. Regulars swear by the huge sandwiches served on chunky rye bread.

9 Xi'an
MAP J5 ■ 362 N Canon Dr
■ 310-275-3345 ■ $$

For a light and tasty take on classic Chinese dishes, head to this stylish place with an outdoor patio. Try the marvelous black bean sauce and the Peking duck.

10 Il Cielo
MAP K5 ■ 9018 Burton Way
■ 310-276-9990 ■ $$$

Book a romantic table beneath a starlit sky in the enchanting garden and enjoy the classic Italian fare.

See map on pp114–15

TOP10 Santa Monica Bay

Detail, Malibu Adamson House

Santa Monica Bay spans 20 miles (32 km) between two of the richest communities in California – Malibu and Palos Verdes. It's truly the "Gold Coast" of the Golden State, and its shores have some of the finest beaches anywhere, including Topanga, Santa Monica, and Venice on through Manhattan, Hermosa, Redondo, and Torrance. American surfing, and the youth culture it spawned, was born here. In the movies, these fabled beaches have stood in for everything from Guadalcanal and Tahiti to Shangri-la. The rows of huge, stately palms along the Santa Monica promenade cliffs epitomize California.

The main attraction, however, is Santa Monica Pier, which offers sundry entertainment options and a lively carnival atmosphere.

SANTA MONICA BAY

Santa Monica Bay

Calabasa

Studio City

Comell

Malibu Creek State Park

Topanga State Park

Monte Nido

Beverly Hills

7 miles (11 km)

Malibu

Malibu Adamson House

Point Dume

see Santa Monica map, right

Santa Monica

Marina del Rey

Inglewood

Los Angeles

El Segundo

Hawthor

Pacific Ocean

South Bay

Redondo Beach

Torran

Top 10 Sights
see pp121–3

Places to Eat
see p127

Unique Boutiques
see p125

Venice Boardwalk Attractions
see p124

Outdoor Pursuits
see p126

Palos Verdes Peninsula

Wayfarer's Chapel

0 km 5
0 miles 5

1 Malibu Adamson House

MAP B2 ■ 23200 Pacific Coast Hwy, Malibu, 310-456-8432 ■ Malibu Lagoon Museum: open 11am–2pm Wed–Thu (tours: 11am–3pm Thu–Sat); adm (free for under 5s) ■ Adamson House: open 11am–3pm Thu–Sun; adm (cash only)

Overlooking the Malibu Lagoon, this Spanish Colonial-style mansion was built by Rhoda Rindge Adamson and her husband Merritt in 1928. The complex showcases hand-painted ceramic tiles manufactured by Malibu Potteries, owned by the Rindge family. The Rindges also built the Malibu Colony, a celebrity enclave where Tom Hanks has a house. The Malibu Lagoon Museum next to the Adamson House chronicles Malibu's history, from its Chumash origins to its position as movie star Shangri-la.

2 Third Street Promenade

MAP B3 ■ 3rd St between Broadway & Wilshire Blvd, Santa Monica

Downtown Santa Monica's main artery, this is one of LA's most pleasant walking areas. The product of a successful revitalization effort in the late 1980s, it is flanked by upscale shops, movie theaters, and restaurants. Street musicians from around the globe perform flamenco, jazz, and hip hop. On Wednesday and Saturday mornings, the farmers' market attracts large crowds.

Third Street Promenade

3 Santa Monica Pier

MAP A3 ■ At the end of Colorado Ave ■ Merry-Go-Round: 310-394-8042, open 11am–5pm daily (until 7pm Fri–Sun) ■ Pacific Park: 310-260-8744 ■ Heal the Bay Aquarium: 310-393-6149

For a variety of entertainment, visit Santa Monica Pier. California's longest operating amusement pier (built in 1908) also marks the western terminus of Route 66. Its oldest attraction is the 1922 Looff Carousel, a historic ride that has made many movie appearances. It is located in Pacific Park, a compact amusement park anchored by a solar-powered Ferris wheel. Tucked beneath the pier, the Heal the Bay Aquarium is a small, family-oriented facility where you can learn about local marine life.

4 Bergamot Station Arts Center

MAP C3 ▪ 2525 Michigan Ave, Santa Monica, 310-586-6488 ▪ Opening hours for galleries vary ▪ www.visit bergamot.com

This former historic trolley station has been renovated into a cultural complex housing nearly three dozen galleries, shops, artists' studios, and a café. A highlight is the City Garage Theatre, which plays host to a variety of cutting-edge contemporary productions round the year. Special events and receptions, designed to keep the community involved in creative processes, are frequently organized by other galleries and businesses in the area. Parking here is free.

Bridge over the Venice Canals

5 Venice Canals

MAP B6 ▪ Between Washington & Venice Blvds

Only 3 miles (5 km) remain of Abbot Kinney's original network of canals. The area, which once languished, has become a beautiful, upscale neighborhood. A narrow walkway that is known as the Venice Canal Walk threads through here.

THE "FATHER OF VENICE"

Venice sprang from the vision of tobacco magnate Abbot Kinney (1850–1920), who transformed the soggy marshland lying south of Santa Monica into a canal-laced, oceanfront theme park complete with gondolas and an amusement pier. It opened on July 4 1905, and was a grand success, until fire destroyed most of the theme park facilities in 1920.

6 Venice Boardwalk

MAP A5 ▪ Ocean Front Walk between Venice Blvd & Rose Ave

It is perhaps fitting that Venice Beach, masterminded by an eccentric visionary named Abbot Kinney, became LA's epicenter of counterculture. The circus-like scene reigning along the seaside boardwalk – officially known as "Ocean Front Walk" – must be seen to be believed (see p124). The area is best avoided after dark.

7 Marina del Rey

MAP B6 ▪ South of Venice Beach ▪ Visitors' Center ▪ 4701 Admiralty Way ▪ 310-305-9545

With 5,000 yachts and pleasure boats, Marina del Rey is the largest small-craft harbor in the world and the place to come for those seeking fun on the water. Active types could explore the harbor on kayaks. You can also catch a dinner cruise, book a whale-watching trip (January to March), or charter a sport fishing boat. A favorite landlubber activity is a sunset dinner at one of the many excellent restaurants.

Picturesque Marina del Rey

8 Wayfarers Chapel

MAP D4 ▪ 5755 Palos
Verdes Dr South ▪ 310-377-7919
▪ Open 9am–5pm daily

The most famous structure by Frank Lloyd Wright is a striking 1951 glass-and-stone memorial to 18th-century theologian Emanuel Swedenborg. The chapel features landscaped grounds, a reflecting pool and terraced amphitheater.

Glazed nave, Wayfarer's Chapel

9 Palos Verdes Peninsula

MAP D5 ▪ Follow Palos Verdes Dr along the coast ▪ Point Vicente Lighthouse: 31501 Palos Verdes Dr West ▪ South Coast Botanic Garden: 26300 Crenshaw Blvd

A drive along the coastline here affords great ocean views with Catalina Island (see pp42–3) in the distance. Malaga Cove and Abalone Cove are popular for their tidepools, and Point Vicente is good for whale-watching. Flower lovers should head to the South Coast Botanic Garden.

10 South Bay

MAP C3

Three picture-perfect beach towns line the southern end of Santa Monica Bay. Of these, Manhattan Beach (see p51) is the most sophisticated, Hermosa (see p51) is the liveliest, and Redondo (see p50) is the most historical. A paved trail parallel to the beach and connecting all the three communities is perfect for bicycling and skating.

A DAY AT THE BEACH

▶ MORNING

Start your day with a drive north along the Pacific Coast Highway for glorious ocean views. Travel to sheltered **Paradise Cove** (Pacific Coast Hwy, Malibu) for breakfast at the pleasant beachfront restaurant, followed by a couple of hours of frolicking in the surf here or a few miles north at **Zuma Beach** (see p50).

Head back south, stopping at **Malibu Adamson House** (see p121) to admire beautiful ceramic tiles before walking over to **Surfrider Beach** (see p50) to watch the world's finest surfers in action.

Then it's off to Santa Monica. Stroll beneath the towering palms of the bluff-top **Palisades Park** (see p53) with the ocean at your feet. For better views of city and sea, treat yourself to a ride on the Ferris wheel on **Santa Monica Pier** (see p121) and perhaps a snack from one of the pier's many vendors.

AFTERNOON

For the rest of the afternoon, rent a bicycle and become part of LA's beach scene during the ride south to Venice along the paved beachfront bike trail. Park the bike or push it along the bizarre **Venice Boardwalk** (see p124), perhaps stopping to get a tattoo (henna or ink), visit a fortune teller, stock up on unique souvenirs, or tank up on wings and local craft beers at **Venice Ale House** (see p124). If time permits, continue south to **Marina del Rey**, one of the world's largest yacht harbors, before heading back to Santa Monica for dinner.

See map on pp120–21 ←

Venice Boardwalk Attractions

1 Windward Avenue
Flanking Windward Avenue are Venice's oldest Renaissance-style buildings, including St. Charles Hotel, a hostel.

2 Sidewalk Café
1401 Ocean Front Walk
■ 310-399-5547
The kitchen produces satisfying sandwiches, salads, and other simple fare. A perfect spot for people-watching.

3 Muscle Beach Venice
Check out bodybuilders with abs of steel at this outdoor gym, successor to the Santa Monica original, which opened in the 1930s.

4 Basketball Courts
The game's always on at Venice's famous outdoor courts, especially during the Venice Basketball League's summer season, which packs the stands on weekends.

5 Street Performers
The best in the business, Boardwalk's street performers dance, perform original songs, dress in costume, and even juggle household objects.

6 Venice Pier
Abbott Kinney built Venice's first pier back in 1905, but the current model dates from 1963. Rescued from demolition in the mid-1980s, the restored fishing pier reopened in 1997.

7 Drum Circle
People of all backgrounds and ages gather on the beach every Saturday and Sunday afternoon, chanting and dancing to the infectious rhythms of pots, bells, and bottles.

8 Beach Architecture
Unique private homes line the Boardwalk between Venice and Washington Boulevards. Look for the one by Steven Ehrlich at No. 2311 and Frank Gehry's eccentric Norton House at No. 2509.

9 Venice Beach Skate Park
2011 Ocean Front Walk
■ 310-822-5639
Watch some of the region's most talented skaters practice tricks in the park, roll around, and capture footage for social media.

10 Murals
Venice Reconstituted, 25 Windward Ave at Speedway ■ Starry Night, Boardwalk at Wavecrest Ave
Numerous murals beautify facades all along the Venice Boardwalk and its side streets. Rip Cronk's *Venice Reconstituted* and *Homage to a Starry Night* are the most famous.

The 700-ft (213-m) Venice Pier

Unique Boutiques

1 **Angel City Books & Records**

MAP B4 ■ 218 Pier Ave, just off Main St ■ 310-399-8767

Bookworms in search of rare and out-of-print books should look no further. A great café next door, too.

2 **Caro Bambino**

MAP B4 ■ 2703 Main St ■ 310-399-7971

Everything for the new parent is sold at this family-owned boutique, from quality natural baby products and toys to stylish toddler apparel, and nursery furniture.

3 **Lost & Found**

MAP B5 ■ 2230 Main St ■ 310-450-9565

An array of clothing and home-ware by independent designers can be found at this shop. Textiles, accessories, candles, and gourmet food items are among the ever-changing stock.

4 **Heist**

MAP B3 ■ 1100 Abbot Kinney Blvd ■ 310-450-6531

A posh, elegant store with a wide selection of designer wear, including riding boots, cozy knits, and slinky dresses on offer.

5 **Burro Venice**

MAP B5 ■ 1409 Abbot Kinney Blvd ■ 310-450-6288

This upscale stationery and houseware store has all the gifts, clothing, and accessories you need to bring home a piece of California.

6 **St. Matthew's Thrift Shop**

MAP B4 ■ 2812 Main St ■ 310-396-9776

Santa Monica's long-standing, Main Street thrift shop is suitable for all budgets. Swing by on the last Saturday of each month for half-price deals.

Gadgets in the jAdis window

7 **jAdis**

MAP B5 ■ 2701 Main St ■ 310-396-3477

A prop- and curiosity shop for sci-fi filmmakers, with spare-part robots, electrical gadgets, Zeppelins, and many other quirky items.

8 **Bazar**

MAP B5 ■ 1108C Abbot Kinney Blvd ■ 310-314-2101

A staple since 1998, Bazar has a rotating blend of vintage clothing, Italian bath products, textiles, furniture, jewelry and European-style decor.

9 **ZJ Boarding House**

MAP B5 ■ 2619 Main St ■ 800-205-7795

This store is for people with a passion for boards – the surf, skate, or snow variety. The knowledgeable staff help to pick through the huge selection of gear.

10 **Mystic Journey Crystals**

MAP B5 ■ 2921 Main St ■ 310-314-0025

Hand-selected crystals and geodes of only the highest quality can be purchased at this vibrant showroom.

See map on pp120–21

Outdoor Pursuits

1 Hiking
Around 500 miles (805 km) of hiking trails meander through the Santa Monica Mountains, stretching from Griffith Park in Hollywood to the north of Malibu. Will Rogers State Historic Park and Topanga State Park are good gateways for hiking.

2 Skating
Enjoy the 22-mile (35-km) Marvin Braude Bike Trail, which runs parallel to the beach from Temescal Canyon Road north of Santa Monica to Torrance Beach.

3 Sailing
Marina Boat Rentals: Fisherman's Village, Marina del Rey, 310-574-2822
Skipper around the marina or cruise out to the open ocean with your very own sailboat. Rental outfits usually have a variety for you to choose from.

4 Boogie Boarding
Enjoy the thrill of the waves on a boogie board – it's easy and fun. All the towns on the beach have rental stations on or near the sand.

5 Bicycling
The paved beach path is equally popular for slow bike cruises. Mountain bikers have plenty to explore in the Santa Monica Mountains.

Bicycling on Venice Boardwalk

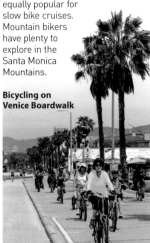

6 Kayaking
One of the nicest places for sea kayaking is off the coast of Catalina Island (see pp42–3). Traveling leisurely by yourself allows you to explore its craggy coastline and to discover your own secret cove.

Surfing off Surfrider Beach

7 Surfing
The archetypal California watersport is practiced all along the coast – Surfrider Beach (see p50) in Malibu is most famous, but Manhattan Beach (see p51) is equally popular.

8 Hang-Gliding
Windsports: 818-367-2430, www.windsports.com
Learn to take to the skies while training on beachside "bunny" hills or launch from a height of 3,500 ft (1,070 m) on a breathtaking flight.

9 Windsurfing
Captain Kirk's (for gear rental & lessons): 310-833-3397
Cabrillo Beach (see p51), nicknamed "Hurricane Gulch," is LA's windsurfing hub. The harbor side is good for beginners, while advanced surfers can make for the open ocean.

10 Fishing
It is permitted to fish without a license off any ocean pier. Sport fishing boats leave from Fisherman's Village in Marina del Rey (see p122), Shoreline Village in Long Beach, and 22nd Street Landing in San Pedro.

Places to Eat

PRICE CATEGORIES

Price categories include a three-course meal for one, a glass of house wine, and all unavoidable extra charges including tax.

$ under $30 $$ $30–$60 $$$ $60–$90
$$$$ over $90

1 Inn of the Seventh Ray
MAP B2 ■ 128 Old Topanga Canyon Rd, off Pacific Coast Hwy ■ 310-455-1311 ■ $$

Tucked away in leafy Topanga Canyon, this creekside retreat offers organic vegetarian, fish, and chicken dishes seasoned with a generous sprinkling of New Age philosophy.

2 Father's Office
MAP C2 ■ 1018 Montana Ave, Santa Monica ■ 310-393-2337 ■ $

This old neighborhood bar has good microbrews and tapas, although regulars swear by the gourmet burger. Delicious fries.

3 Pasjoli
MAP B4 ■ 2732 Main St ■ 424-330-0020 ■ $$$$

Seasonal local produce, a wide wine cellar, and classic French bistro cuisine are the stars at this stylish spot. The pressed duck is a standout on the menu.

4 Michael's
MAP B3 ■ 1147 3rd St, Santa Monica ■ 310-451-0843 ■ $$$$

The romantic garden is a luscious setting for Oscar-worthy Californian cuisine and spot-on service.

5 Chinois on Main
MAP B4 ■ 2709 Main St, Santa Monica ■ 310-392-9025 ■ $$$

A Franco-Chinese menu includes Cantonese duck in plum sauce. Jacket and tie required.

6 Tender Greens
MAP B3 ■ 201 Arizona Ave ■ 310-587-2777 ■ $

Healthy, fresh food sourced from local farmers is the emphasis at this growing chain. Order at the counter and take a seat. Favorites include the albacore sandwich, the kale salad, and the falafel wrap.

7 Fritto Misto
MAP A4 ■ 601 Colorado Blvd ■ 310-458-2829 ■ $$

Come hungry to this friendly Italian café. Pasta-lovers will delight at the "create your own pasta" option. Choose a pasta, a sauce, and some add ins and expect perfection.

8 1212 Santa Monica
MAP B3 ■ 1212 Third St Promenade ■ 310-576-9996 ■ $$$

An open, airy restaurant that serves "new California" cuisine made with fresh produce and innovative cocktails. It's a great spot for people-watching.

Chef Rafael Lunetta at work, Mélisse

9 Mélisse and Citrin
MAP B3 ■ 1104 Wilshire Blvd, Santa Monica ■ 310-395-0881 ■ $$$$

This two-Michelin-starred dining spot offers two distinct concepts: a 14-seat restaurant called Mélisse and an upscale bistro called Citrin.

10 Eat At Joe's
MAP D4 ■ 400 N Pacific Coast Hwy, Redondo Beach ■ 310-376-9570 ■ $

A friendly diner serving large portions of American comfort food.

See map on pp120–21

▣⑩ Coastal Orange County

Rent a convertible, put the top down, and turn the radio up. Pacific Coast Highway (or PCH as the locals call it) runs 42 miles (68 km) alongside sweeping stretches of beach with vast ocean views and secluded coves with tide pools bursting with marine life. Come here to have fun and experience the sun-drenched coastal lifestyle. Sometimes called the "California Riviera" for its palatial five-star hotels, multimillion dollar homes, and yacht harbors, Orange County (OC) also has charming cottages, gardens, and communities that haven't changed much in the last 50 years. You can walk on piers, ride an old-fashioned Ferris wheel, admire surfers, stroll through art galleries, splash in the water, watch passersby from sidewalk cafés, or simply gaze out over the ocean.

Seafront properties in the beach town of San Clemente

COASTAL ORANGE COUNTY

1 San Clemente

Center stage in the late 1960s and early 1970s as the location of "the Western White House" during the Nixon presidency, San Clemente still has the feeling of a normal, non-touristy California beach town. Downtown is filled with affordable restaurants and cafés, as well as antiques, apparel, and gift shops. The town's main attraction, though, is its clean sandy beach and pier. At the far south end of town, surfers rate the Trestles spots as some of the best on this stretch of coast.

2 Bolsa Chica Ecological Reserve

MAP F5 ▪ Huntington Beach ▪ www. bolsachica.org

A world away from the coastal beach culture, this preserve is a wonderful place to walk. An easy 1.5-mile (2.4-km) trail loops through 2 sq miles (5 sq km) of restored salt marsh (one of Southern California's largest), lowlands, and mesa, which are home to over 300 species of migratory birds. Displays point out the varieties of herons, egrets, plovers, terns, and ospreys that roost here, as well as the mussels, clams, and 80 species of fish present.

3 Huntington Beach

Known as "Surf City USA" in no small part because of the consistent waves that break along 8 miles (13 km) of uninterrupted sand beach, Huntington Beach is home to the world's largest surfing

competition and to the International Surfing Museum. Generally, it's a young crowd that comes here to hit the beach and surf during the day, and to enjoy a meal and a drink at night. Huntington has traditionally been far more affordable than other beach towns further down the coast.

Tide pools, Crystal Cove State Park

4 Crystal Cove State Park

MAP G6 ▪ 8471 Pacific Coast Hwy, Laguna Beach ▪ www. crystalcovestatepark.org

Over 3 miles (5 km) of unspoiled shoreline, tide pools, and secluded coves are yours to explore here. Offshore, you may see a pod of dolphins frolicking by or even a few California gray whales. Along part of the beach, 45 vintage cottages (many of which you can rent) make up the Crystal Cove Historic District, which exemplifies early 20th-century coastal living. Across the Pacific Coast Highway, numerous back-country trails are open to hikers and mountain bikers.

5 Seal Beach

Head to this low-key ocean playground just south of the San Gabriel River for a taste of small-town America. On tree-lined Main Street you'll find cafés and restaurants. Don't miss walking out on Seal Beach's classic 1,865-ft (570-m) wooden fishing pier. Warm waters and small to mid-size waves make it ideal for swimmers and surfers, while kite surfers flock here for the consistent breeze.

Surfing off Huntington Beach

THAT WORTHLESS COASTAL LAND

From 1784 to 1846, the governments of Spain and Mexico awarded vast tracts of land in reward for military service and to encourage settlement. Most of Orange County belonged to this "rancho" system except for Laguna Beach, its rocky coastline deemed unusable. Nowadays, ocean-front properties in that useless coastal land (**below**) are selling for $30 million.

6 Balboa Island

This coveted piece of OC real estate holds one of the most charming villages of Newport Beach. Cottages are densely packed on narrow streets bearing the name of precious stones. Restaurants, galleries, and boutiques line either side of Marine Avenue, Balboa Island's main shopping street.

7 Laguna Beach

Maybe it's for the light – so similar to that of the south of France – or the romantic secluded coves or the way the hillsides tumble down to the sea that artists have been drawn to the spectacular setting that is Laguna Beach for over 100 years. It is still very much an art town, although skyrocketing real-estate prices have changed the town's character. You'll still find quaint cottages with flower-filled gardens on side streets, charming arcades with tiny shops, and a gorgeous coastline.

8 Dana Point

MAP G6 ■ Captain Dave's Dolphin and Whale Watching Safari: www.dolphinsafari.com

Richard Henry Dana wrote in his epic 19th-century book *Two Years Before the Mast* that this area was one the most beautiful spots on this stretch of coast. Today, Dana Point has a vague New England look in homage to its namesake and a harbor busy with activities, including kayaking, paddle boarding, and tide pooling. Because of its unique offshore geology, the ocean here has one of the world's richest marine mammal environments. Don't miss a trip on Captain Dave's Dolphin and Whale Watching Safari, a catamaran excursion taking you up close to whales and dolphins.

9 Mission San Juan Capistrano

MAP H6 ■ 26801 Ortega Hwy, San Juan Capistrano ■ www.missionsjc.com

The seventh in a chain of 21 Spanish missions, this was known as the "Jewel of the Missions." To cement Spanish rule in the land, the missions worked to "assimilate" the Indigenous Acjachemen people, whose land they were taking, by forcing them to join the missions and change their culture, language, diet, religion, and clothing. Living in the missions meant that the community was fatally exposed to diseases brought over by the Spanish, such as measles, tuberculosis, and

Mission San Juan Capistrano

pneumonia. The decimation of the Indigenous population, and the 1812 earthquake that destroyed the Great Stone Church, contributed to Mission San Juan Capistrano's decline in the 1800s. Today, the ruins of the Great Stone Church can still be seen at the mission, along with a number of exhibition galleries detailing the complex's history.

⑩ Newport Beach

Few towns can outdo Newport Beach for making a grandiose first impression. Mega-yachts tie up side by side in its harbor; luxury car dealerships line the Coast Highway, and mansions perch on the hillsides. Spread out along the coast and into the hills, Newport Beach consists of several distinct areas, such as the down-to-earth Balboa Peninsula with a boardwalk that's popular with walkers and cyclists, and European-style Corona del Mar filled with trendy shops and upscale restaurants.

The scenic Newport Beach

A DAY IN BALBOA

▶ MORNING

Begin your day on the bridge leading over to **Balboa Island**. Stroll down **Marine Avenue** checking out the boutiques and cafés. A dedicated pedestrian sidewalk wends its way around the entire circumference of the island. To your left is the harbor filled with sailboats, yachts, and canopied electric boats. To your right the sidewalk is lined with delightful cottages and gardens. After half a mile (1 km) is the **Balboa Island Ferry** *(510 Palm St)*. Operating since 1919, the ferry carries three cars, bicyclists, and pedestrians across the harbor to the Balboa Peninsula. Ride the ferry to the **Balboa Fun Zone**. Take a ride on the Ferris Wheel for a great view of the harbor. At the Fun Zone Boat Company, one 45-minute harbor tour passes by the yachts and mansions and another goes out to the harbor entrance, where you'll see sea lions. A good lunch option is **Ruby's Diner** *(949-675-7829)* at the end of 1 Balboa Pier.

AFTERNOON

After lunch, rent a beach cruiser bicycle and ride along the 3-mile (5-km) long boardwalk between two piers on the beach side of the Peninsula. Spend your afternoon enjoying the friendly beach town. At the end of the day back on Marine Avenue, reward yourself with a chocolate-covered frozen banana from one of the shops on the right-hand side of the street. They've been making them there since 1945.

See map on p128

Art Experiences in Laguna Beach

1 Festival of Arts and Pageant of the Masters

MAP G6 ▪ 650 Laguna Canyon Rd ▪ 949-494-1145 ▪ Jul–Aug ▪ www. foapom.com

This festival showcases the art of over 140 local artists. In an amphitheater, live models, elaborate sets, and an orchestra re-create famous paintings.

Sawdust Art Festival stall

2 Sawdust Art Festival

MAP G6 ▪ 935 Laguna Canyon Rd ▪ 949-494-3030 ▪ Jun–Aug ▪ www.sawdustartfestival.org

Laguna Beach artists exhibit original handmade crafts, and there are artist demonstrations and live music.

3 Laguna College of Art and Design Gallery

MAP G6 ▪ 374 Ocean Ave ▪ 949-376-6000 ▪ Open 11am–4pm Wed–Sun ▪ www.lcad.edu

Students from this highly regarded art college display their works in a downtown gallery open to the public.

4 Laguna Art Museum

MAP G6 ▪ 307 Cliff Dr ▪ 949-494-8971 ▪ Open 10am–5pm Tue–Sun ▪ Adm ▪ www. lagunaartmuseum.org

The focus is on Californian art, with a vast collection of works from the early 19th century to the present.

5 First Thursdays Art Walk

www.firstthursdaysartwalk.org

On the first Thursday of every month, galleries hold demonstrations, receptions, and, often, live music.

6 Public Art

Over 100 pieces of public art are on display throughout town. Be on the lookout in Heisler Park, the Coast Highway, or downtown.

7 Dawson Cole Fine Art

MAP G6 ▪ 326 Glenneyre St ▪ 949-497-4988 ▪ Open 11am–5pm daily ▪ www.dawsoncolefineart.com

Come here to view the exquisite bronze sculptures of contemporary figurative artist Richard MacDonald. Don't miss the sculpture garden.

8 Redfern Gallery

MAP G6 ▪ 1540 S Coast Hwy ▪ 949-497-3356 ▪ Open 10am–5pm Tue–Sat ▪ www.redferngallery.com

American Impressionists with an emphasis on early California *plein air* artists, such as William Wendt and Edgar Payne, are exhibited here.

9 Wyland Galleries

MAP G6 ▪ 509 S Coast Hwy ▪ 949-376-8000 ▪ Open 9am–8pm daily ▪ www.wyland.com

Marine artist Robert Wyland painted his first of 100 outdoor whaling walls just next door. On sale are original paintings, prints, and sculptures.

10 John Barber Glass Designs

MAP G6 ▪ 21062 Laguna Cyn Rd ▪ 949-494-1464 ▪ Opening hours vary, check website ▪ johnbarberglassdesigns.com

Tucked in a wooded area of Laguna Canyon, the studio and showroom of this master glass blower is a fantastic glimpse into an artist's world. Pieces are quite affordable.

Places to Eat

1 25 Degrees
MAP F5 ■ 412 Walnut Ave, Huntington Beach ■ 714-960-2525 ■ $$

High-end gourmet burgers are fashioned to your desire. Choose from ground sirloin, tuna, turkey, or veggie and go from there. Garlic fries are a must, as is a spiked milkshake.

2 The Beachcomber Cafe
MAP G6 ■ 15 Crystal Cove, Newport Coast ■ 949-376-6900 ■ $$

Soak in the ocean view with coconut macadamia pancakes for breakfast or watch the sunset with a Tiki drink at this prime-location café.

3 Mastro's Ocean Club
MAP F5 ■ 8112 East Coast Hwy, Newport Beach ■ 949-376-6990 ■ $$$

Romantic and sophisticated, Maestro offers steak and seafood cooked to perfection. Start with a seafood tower made to order and finish with their famous warm butter cake.

4 Zinc Café & Market
MAP G6 ■ 350 Ocean Ave, Laguna Beach ■ 949-494-6302 ■ $

Claim a table in the outdoor patio and order your food at the counter at this popular café. Vegetarians will love the choices – everything from potato enchiladas to avocado toast.

5 Las Brisas
MAP G6 ■ 361 Cliff Dr, Laguna Beach ■ 949-497-5434 ■ $$

Mexican seafood with a California twist is the main feature here, along with its breathtaking coastal

The patio at Las Brisas

views – you can't go wrong for breakfast, lunch, or dinner. The patio is the place for margaritas.

6 Splashes
MAP G6 ■ 1555 S Coast Hwy, Laguna Beach ■ 877-741-5908 ■ $$$

Situated just off the beach at the Surf & Sand Resort, Splashes is elegant yet casual and very romantic. Breakfasts are excellent but pricey.

7 Mozambique
MAP G6 ■ 1740 S Coast Hwy ■ 949-715-7777 ■ $$$

Gorgeous dining rooms provide the ambience for excellent Southern African dishes. The rooftop hosts the best happy hour in Laguna Beach.

8 La Sirena Grill
MAP G6 ■ 30862 S Coast Hwy, Laguna Beach ■ 949-499-2301 ■ $

A favorite with locals, this is the place for fresh, well-prepared Mexican food. Calamari tacos are excellent, as are the veggie enchiladas. Twenty craft beers are on tap.

9 Ramos House Café
MAP H6 ■ 31752 Los Rio St, San Juan Capistrano ■ 949-443-1342 ■ $$

In a 19th-century home in the Rios District, the Ramos House serves a delicious brunch. The smoked bacon scramble and apple cinnamon beignets are especially tasty.

10 The Fisherman's Restaurant & Bar
MAP H7 ■ 611 Avenida Victoria, San Clemente ■ 949-498-6390 ■ $$

Situated at the base of the town pier, the most coveted tables overlook the ocean. Enjoy seafood while watching the surfers with the sunset beyond.

See map on p128

Streetsmart

Mural behind the Hollywood Wax
Museum, Hollywood Boulevard

Getting Around

Arriving by Air

Five main airports serve the region: **Los Angeles International (LAX)**, **Hollywood Burbank Airport**, **Long Beach Airport**, **Ontario International Airport**, and Santa Ana/Orange County's **John Wayne Airport**.

Nearly 70 airlines serve LAX, making it one of the world's busiest airports.

Compared to using other major world airports, arriving at and leaving LAX can be confusing. When exiting baggage claim, color-coded signs indicate where you need to wait depending on where you are going and by what mode of transport. Rental cars, shuttles, shared ride vans, buses, and taxis, as well as hotels, have different colored signs. Pink indicates the LAX bus connectors, with one route that continuously circles the terminals, another that goes to the City Bus Center, and a third that takes you to the nearby Metro rail line at the Aviation/LAX Station.

Green signs indicate the LAX-it lot, the off-site meeting space where all taxi and rideshare trips from the airport originate.

Red signs signal hotel and private parking shuttles. Purple is for rental car companies. Blue signs indicate the LAX Flyaway, which takes you directly to Van Nuys or Union Station.

A short drive down the highway from Hollywood, Hollywood Burbank Airport is served by eight airlines in two terminals. Metrolink and Amtrak stop across the street at a small station.

Ontario International Airport is located just 38 miles (61 km) east of downtown LA and offers some international flights to South America and Asia.

Just south of LA, Long Beach Airport offers a range of connections to major US destinations.

John Wayne Airport has limited international flights from Vancouver, Canada, and a few cities in Mexico.

Regional Trains

Amtrak trains arriving at the historic Union Station in Downtown include the Coast Starlight from Seattle, the Southwest Chief from Chicago, and the Sunset Limited from New Orleans.

Metrolink, a regional commuter rail system, connects LA to Anaheim and stops further south in Orange County. Another useful line goes from Union Station to Burbank and the San Fernando Valley. Metrolink trains operate from the early morning into the evening.

Public Transportation

LA Metro, LA's main transportation authority, runs the city's bus and train networks. Safety and hygiene measures, timetables, ticket information, and transport maps can be obtained from the LA Metro website. Bikes can be transported on Metrolink trains and LA Metro trains and buses.

Trains can get busy heading into Downtown weekday mornings between 7:30am and 9am, but LA rush-hour traffic (running from 5am–9am and 3–7pm Monday to Friday) is far worse. Taking Metro trains is much faster than using buses and cars during the day.

Tickets

To ride the Metro Rail, you must have a **TAP Card** ($2) – which can also be used on the city's bus network. Cards can be purchased in any Metro Rail station or from vendors in popular tourist areas. You can download the TAP app for iPhones and Android phones for contactless payment. You can store value or add a 1-, 7-, or 30-day pass to the card or app (use any stored value before loading a pass). A regular fare of $1.75 allows two hours of unlimited transfers in one direction. Buses also accept cash, but exact fare only.

Metro Rail

LA Metro operates six lines that stretch from one end of the county to the other, across around 100 stations. The B Line, the city's only subway route, goes from Union Station to North Hollywood via Universal City. The D Line, which will get an extension in 2025, parallels this as far as Wilshire/Vermont then goes on to Wilshire/ Western. The A Line travels from downtown Long Beach all the way to Pasadena and beyond

(APU/Citrus College), while the E Line runs from downtown Santa Monica to East LA. The C Line crosses LA from Norwalk to El Segundo (Aviation Station for LAX), and Redondo Beach. The K Line runs from Expo/Crenshaw to Westchester/Veterans with plans to expand to Aviation/LAX Station in the future.

Metro Rail trains run daily from 5am to midnight (until 2am Fri & Sat), every five minutes during peak hours and every 10–15min at other times.

All Metro Rail lines are wheelchair-accessible.

Long-Distance Bus Travel

Greyhound operates a huge network of air-conditioned coaches all across the US. Bus travel is inexpensive but can be slow and is mainly recommended if you're arriving from nearby cities such as San Francisco or Las Vegas. Buses stop at the main Greyhound terminal in LA's Downtown area. Although walk-up ticket sales are readily available, Greyhound offers substantial discounts for purchasing tickets online and in advance.

Megabus connects with Las Vegas, stopping at Union Station's Patsaouras Transit Plaza. Tickets must be booked online and are not sold by the driver or on the bus.

Buses

The LA Metro bus network covers just about anywhere you want to go in LA, if you have the time.

For visitors, the most useful routes are those running from Downtown to Santa Monica, Beverly Hills, and Hollywood. If paying with cash, standard one-ride bus fares are $1.75 with no transfers – exact change must be used. If paying with a TAP Card/app, two hours of unlimited transfers are included in the fare price.

Santa Monica operates its own bus network, the **Big Blue Bus**. Especially useful routes for visitors are the Rapid #10, between Santa Monica and Downtown, the #3, from Santa Monica to the LAX area, and the #1 between Santa Monica and Venice Beach. Fares are $1.10, but you must use the TAP Card or TAP app to pay – no cash accepted.

DASH buses provide a frequent service to Union Station, Chinatown, Little Tokyo, the Fashion District, LA Live, and the Music Center. Fares are just 50¢ cash, or just 35¢ using a TAP Card/app.

All buses feature wheelchair lifts or ramps.

Taxis

Getting around town by taxi can be a pricey proposition unless you're traveling as a group or are only going a short distance. Taxi drivers usually won't respond to being hailed but must be ordered in advance, from **United Checker Cab, Independent Cab, LA City Cab,** or **Yellow Cab.** Taxis are recognizable by the official City of Los Angeles Taxicab Seal on the car door. The ride-sharing services Uber and Lyft also operates in the city.

DIRECTORY

ARRIVING BY AIR

Hollywood Burbank Airport
w hollywoodburbank airport.com

John Wayne Airport
w ocair.com

Long Beach Airport
w lgb.org

Los Angeles International (LAX)
w flylax.com

Ontario International Airport
w flyontario.com

REGIONAL TRAINS

Amtrak
w amtrak.com

Metrolink
w metrolinktrains.com

PUBLIC TRANSPORTATION

LA Metro
w metro.net

TICKETS

TAP Card
w taptogo.net

LONG-DISTANCE BUS TRAVEL

Flix Bus
w flixbus.com

Greyhound
w greyhound.com

Megabus
w us.megabus.com

BUSES

Big Blue Bus
w bigbluebus.com

DASH
w ladottransit.com/dash

TAXIS

Independent Cab
c 800-521-8294

LA City Cab
c 888-248-9222

United Checker Cab
c 877-201-8294

Yellow Cab
c 424-222-2222

Driving to Los Angeles

Driving is a great way to explore California, though distances are vast and freeways can be challenging. Several freeways lead straight to and through LA, including the I-5, Hwy 101, and I-405 from the north; the I-10 from the east; and the I-5 and I-405 from the south. Try to time your arrival in LA to avoid the morning rush-hour traffic from 5am to 9am.

Toll Roads

There are a number of toll roads in and around LA. These tolls are collected electronically – there are no toll booths at which to stop and pay. If you drive on a toll road without an electronic pass, you face a hefty fine and administration fees from your rental company. Your car may be fitted with an electronic pass, but using this may incur a daily fee from the rental company (plus tolls incurred), regardless of usage – make sure you understand the billing structure before you drive off. If you expect to be driving on toll roads a lot, it may be worth buying a transponder (an electronic toll collector) from **FasTrak**.

Car Rental

Foreign drivers' licenses are valid in the US, but if your license is not in English, you must get an International Driver's License. Drivers must have held their licenses for at least one year, and visitors under 25 years of age may encounter restrictions when renting, usually having to pay an extra $20–30 a day (check in advance). If you're under 21, you will usually not be able to rent a car at all (there are some exemptions, but usually only for US license holders, and then with a hefty surcharge).

Unlike most US states, in California all additional drivers are free. You must still list the additional driver on the contract.

All major rental car companies including **Alamo**, **Avis**, **Budget**, **Enterprise**, **Hertz**, and **Sixt** are represented at LAX. Rentals are easily arranged before arriving in California. When picking up your rental car, you may be asked to show your passport and return airline ticket – you will also need a credit card.

Most rental companies offer GPS (SatNav) for an additional daily fee, and child seats with advance notice. Free unlimited mileage is often included, but leaving the car in a different city than the one in which you rent it may incur a substantial drop-off fee. Standard rental cars in the US have automatic transmissions.

Be sure to check for any pre-existing damage to the car and note this on your contract before you leave the rental lot.

Car Insurance

When you rent a car in California you will be asked to add on an array of insurance extras. California requires you have at least some type of liability insurance. Note that the rental company is not required to enforce this and may assume you are covered by your own policy. Complying with California's law on rental car insurance is the responsibility of the renter. In brief, loss-damage waiver (LDW) or collision damage waiver (CDW) means you avoid paying for any damage to the rental vehicle or theft of the car. However, there are sometimes "minimums" as opposed to "full" coverage, which can mean you are liable for the first $1,000 of damage, for example. Punctured tires and windshield (windscreen) damage are often not covered. Supplemental liability protection (SLP) will pay for damage you cause to other drivers' vehicles or property – again, check how much this actually covers. Personal accident insurance covers medical costs if the car is involved in an accident. In general it's a good idea to take at least LDW plus SLP – even a minor accident can result in astronomical costs. Check if your own car insurance will cover rentals.

Driving in Los Angeles

Driving in LA is generally not recommended – roads are congested in the city-center and parking can be very difficult to find. Visitors may find that taking the Metro Rail is quicker and cheaper than driving through the city. Always allow plenty of time, especially during the morning and evening rush hours when gridlock is common.

Rules of the Road

Everywhere in California (and throughout the US) driving is on the right-hand side of the road, and all distances are measured in miles. Seat belts are compulsory. Right turns on a red traffic light (unless otherwise indicated) are allowed after coming to a complete stop. All vehicles must give way to emergency service vehicles, and traffic in both directions must stop for a school bus when signals flash.

California prohibits the use of mobile phones while driving, with the exception of a "hands-free" system. Speeding will usually result in a fine which you should pay in person if possible – if you are renting the car, the rental company will otherwise charge you hefty additional administration fees.

Driving under the influence of alcohol or cannabis is a very serious offence, likely leading to arrest. It is illegal for any person aged 21 or over to drive a car if their BAC (blood alcohol content) level is 0.08 per cent or higher.

If you suffer a breakdown, call the American Automobile Association (AAA) for help.

Parking

Drivers should study all parking restriction signs, including what's posted on the meter as you'll often find information in different spots. LA has paid on-and off-street parking with parking meters and designated car parks (parking lots). Parking in Downtown is usually very expensive – you should factor this into your daily costs. Hotels can charge $25–60 per day for on-site parking.

Parking enforcement is aggressive. Illegally parked cars run the risk of being towed with a substantial fine.

Cycle and Scooter Hire

The good news is LA is mostly flat, while the bad news is you're competing for road space with heavy traffic. LA has nearly 600 miles (965 km) of bikeways, which is increasing with the growing popularity of biking. While experienced cyclists may feel comfortable navigating LA's city centre, those less confident on a bike may prefer cycling along the quieter coast from Santa Monica to Redondo Beach, and from Long Beach to Newport Beach in Orange County.

All buses in LA County are equipped with front racks for passengers to carry bicycles. Cyclists under age 18 must wear a helmet by law.

Metro Bike Share in LA is a bike-share program with docking stations in downtown, Central LA, and North Hollywood that allow cyclists to make one-way bike trips for a nominal fee. Alternatively, **Bird** is a GPS-powered dockless system that offers e-bikes and scooters. **Lyft** and **Lime** also offer electric bikes and scooters which can be picked up in various locations around the city (check online for more information).

Walking

Though it may not be feasible to tackle the entirety of this sprawling city on foot, many areas in LA are walkable. Beverly Hills, Santa Monica, Hollywood, Downtown, Venice, and Pasadena are all very pedestrian-friendly, with some of the top sights within walking distance of each other. Pedestrians have the right of way at crossings.

DIRECTORY

TOLL ROADS

FasTrack
w fastrack.org

CAR RENTAL

Alamo
w alamo.com

Avis
w avis.com

Budget
w budget.com

Enterprise
w enterprise.com

Hertz
w hertz.co.uk

Sixt
w sixt.co.uk

RULES OF THE ROAD

AAA
📞 800 222 4357
w aaa.com

CYCLE AND SCOOTER HIRE

Bird
w bird.co

Lime
w li.me

Lyft
w lyft.com

Metro Bike Share
w bikeshare.metro.net

Practical Information

Passports and Visas

For entry requirements, including visas, consult your nearest United States embassy or check the **US State Department** website. All visitors to the US must have a valid passport. Citizens of 39 countries, including Australia, New Zealand, and the UK, may enter visa free under the Visa Waver Program for stays of up to 90 days. To use this program you must have an e-Passport with an electronic chip and apply for eligibility through ESTA (Electronic System for Travel Authorization) prior to travel. Visitors from all other regions will require a tourist visa and passport to enter. A return airline ticket is also required to enter the US.

Government Advice

Now more than ever, it is important to consult both your and the United States government's advice before traveling. The **UK Foreign and Commonwealth Office**, the **Australian Department of Foreign Affairs and Trade**, and the US State Department offer the latest information on security, health, and local regulations.

Customs Information

You can find information on the laws relating to goods and currency taken in or out of the United States on the **US Customs and Border Protection** website. Clearing customs and immigration at LAX can be a long procedure as even transit passengers must be processed.

Everyone over the age of 21 is allowed a liter of liquor and 200 cigarettes duty free. US citizens may bring in $400 worth of gifts and non-US citizens only $100. Cash over the value of $10,000 needs to be declared. Fresh meat, plants, and products from any endangered species are prohibited.

Insurance

We recommend that you take out a comprehensive insurance policy, covering theft, loss of belongings, medical care, cancellations, and delays, and read the small print carefully. There is no universal healthcare in the United States for citizens or visitors and healthcare is very expensive so it is particularly important to take out comprehensive medical insurance.

Health

The United States has a world-class, private health care system. Urgent care clinics accept patients on a walk-in basis, though you can expect to pay for services before treatment. Call your insurance company for a referral to a local doctor. Keep all medical receipts for reimbursement later.

Major drugstores such as **CVS**, **Walgreens**, and **Rite Aid** have full-service pharmacies, most of which keep late hours (some are open 24 hours a day). If you take prescription drugs, it's best to bring your own supply.

For information regarding COVID-19 vaccination requirements, consult government advice.

Unless otherwise stated, tap water is safe to drink.

Although air quality has improved dramatically, sensitive lungs can feel air pollution on certain days, especially the further inland you are.

Ocean waters are generally clean, except for three days after a heavy storm when untreated runoff washes down storm drains and empties into the ocean, and sewer leaks are common. Avoid swimming at these times.

Dangerous riptides can occur along the coast. Posted green flags indicate safe swimming, yellow mean caution, and red flags denote hazardous surf. If you are caught in a riptide, let the current carry you down the coast until it dies out, and then swim in to shore.

Smoking, Alcohol, and Drugs

You must be at least 21 years of age to drink or purchase alcohol or buy cigarettes and any other tobacco products in the US; expect to show photo ID even if you look much older.

In California smoking is banned in all indoor public places, including restaurants, bars, and hotels, and in many outdoor public spaces, such as all public parks, beaches, and any pedestrian plazas.

US Federal law prohibits the use of cannabis, but California has legalized limited amounts of 1 ounce (8g) for recreational use for anyone over the age of 21, including visitors. However, it is illegal to smoke cannabis in public places, including on transport or in hotels and hostels. Taking any amount of cannabis across state lines or international borders is highly illegal, and being caught doing this or being in possession of any other drug will likely result in a jail sentence.

ID

There is no requirement for visitors to carry ID, but due to occasional checks (especially at Federal sites) you may be asked to show a passport or other picture ID.

Personal Security

Although much of LA is safe for visitors, there are areas, as in any city, that may not be especially tourist friendly. Use common sense and be aware of your surroundings – particularly in crowded areas like Venice Beach or Hollywood Boulevard – and you should enjoy a stress free trip Never leave items visible in your car; consider leaving valuables in a safe place at your hotel.

If you have lost something on a Metro Bus or Rail, allow about three days for your property to be logged into the **Lost and Found** system. Dial

911 for **ambulance**, **fire**, or **police**. In a serious emergency, medical assistance is available 24 hours a day in hospital emergency rooms. Contact your embassy if you have your passport stolen, or in the event of a serious crime or accident.

California has one of the most multicultural and diverse populations in the US and has a long history of celebrating LGBTQ+ rights. California recognized the rights of those wanting to legally change their gender in the mid-1980s and same-sex marriage was legalized in 2008. The main LGBTQ+ center in LA is the **LA LGBT Center**.

Travelers with Specific Requirements

Los Angeles is a relatively accessible place for those with visual, mobility, or hearing impairments.

By law, all public buildings, museums, and restaurants must have wheelchair access. Sidewalk curbs are cut to facilitate movement, hotels have rooms with extra wide doors, and car-rental agencies offer special hand-controlled cars. Buses are equipped with wheelchair lifts and all LA Metro Rail stations are wheelchair accessible.

Many museums and galleries such as The Getty Center and LACMA offer visual description audio tours for those with visual impairments; the Getty Center also offers text transcriptions of audio tours.

Both Disneyland® Resort and Universal

Studios Hollywood℠ offer sign language interpretation and audio description services for visitors with specific requirements.

Discover Los Angeles features an informative online guide detailing the range of accessibility services in LA.

DIRECTORY

PASSPORTS AND VISAS

US State Department
Ⓦ travel.state.gov

GOVERNMENT ADVICE

Australian Department of Foreign Affairs and Trade
Ⓦ smartraveller.gov.au

UK Foreign and Commonwealth Office
Ⓦ gov.uk/foreign-travel-advice

CUSTOMS INFORMATION

US Customs and Border Protection
Ⓦ cbp.gov

HEALTH

CVS
Ⓦ cvs.com

Rite Aid
Ⓦ riteaid.com

Walgreens
Ⓦ walgreens.com

PERSONAL SECURITY

Ambulance, Fire, Police
Ⓒ 911

LA LGBT Center
Ⓦ lalgbtcenter.org

Lost and Found
Ⓦ lostandfound.metro.net

TRAVELERS WITH SPECIFIC REQUIREMENTS

Discover Los Angeles
Ⓦ discoverlosangeles.com

Time Zone

From the first Sunday in November until the second Sunday in March, LA operates on Pacific Standard Time (PST).

For the remaining months the clock moves ahead one hour and becomes Pacific Daylight Time (PDT).

Money

The US currency is the dollar ($), which is divided into 100 cents.

LAX has international exchange kiosks, but rates are usually not competitive. **LA Currency** offers good rates and has locations in Downtown and in Hollywood. Large hotels often exchange currency as well, but often offer bad rates.

Most major banks can be found in LA; they handle a range of transactions, but customers must bring at least two forms of ID with them.

Major credit and debit cards, including American Express, are widely accepted, as are prepaid currency cards and Apple Pay. ATMs are common though most charge a fee of $1–$3 per transaction.

In restaurants it is normal to tip 15–20 per cent of the total bill. Allow for a tip of 15 per cent for taxi drivers and bar staff. Hotel porters and housekeeping expect $1–$2 per bag or day.

Electrical Appliances

Electrical appliances in the US operate on 110–120 volts and use two-prong plugs. Non-US, single-voltage appliances need a transformer and an adapter, commonly available at airport shops, electrical stores, and large department stores.

Cell Phones and Wi-Fi

Fast speed internet and Wi-Fi is available in cafés, fast-food restaurants, shopping centers, and bookstores all over the city. Public libraries usually also have computer terminals to use, as do hostels, but you must be a guest. Most hotels offer free Wi-Fi, as does LAX. High-end hotels usually charge for internet access.

Local SIM cards, purchased from US providers such as **AT&T**, can be used in compatible phones. Canadian residents can usually upgrade their domestic cell phone plan to extend to the US.

Postal Services

US Postal Services (**USPS**) runs the postal system in the US. Depending on the branch, post office hours are 8:30am to 5pm Monday to Friday, with some branches open on Saturday mornings. Post offices can be found throughout the city.

Stamps are usually available from vending machines in the lobby, and signage indicates the cost of postage for mail sent to domestic and international addresses. Stamps can also be found at many supermarkets and franchised mail service stores, which also provide shipping services. Hotel concierges can post mail for you.

FedEx and **UPS** offer courier services with guaranteed overnight delivery and reliable international service. Much cheaper, USPS offers overnight service in the continental US and two- and three-day service internationally.

Weather

LA has a moderate climate with low humidity and cool evenings, even in summer. Rain is most likely from January to March. Late spring often presents what locals call "May gray" and "June gloom," when low cloud cover never seems to end, but just as easily you can get endless days of sun.

Summer is the busiest time of year, with warm days and cool yet pleasant evenings on the coast. Further inland, the temperatures soar, making any time spent outdoors uncomfortable. Showers during this time of year are incredibly rare.

Opening Hours

Most museums are open from 10am to 5pm. Always check the website or call before making plans, since many close one day out of the week.

Stores usually open at 10am and close between 5 and 6pm. Regular hours at malls are 10am to 9pm Monday to Saturday and 11am to 7pm Sunday. Department stores sometimes open at 7am for super sales or extend their hours during the holiday season. Malls close only during a few major holidays, such as Christmas and New Years; however, some stores may be open on Thanksgiving (the fourth Thursday in November) and Easter Sunday.

Banking hours are usually from 9 or 10am to 6pm Monday to Friday, with Saturday hours from 9am to 1 or 2pm.

You shouldn't have any trouble finding 24-hour convenience stores, gas stations, drug stores, and supermarkets in and around LA.

Situations can change quickly and unexpectedly. Always check before visiting attractions and hospitality venues for up-to-date opening hours and booking requirements.

Visitor Information

The **LA Tourism and Convention Board** website offers a wealth of information. In addition, there are organizations such as **Santa Monica Convention and Visitors' Bureau**, **Beverly Hills Visitors' Bureau**, and **Pasadena Visitors' Bureau**.

Go City passes offer up to 50 per cent off most attractions in LA.

Responsible Tourism

The climate crisis is having a big impact on Los Angeles, with droughts and heatwaves becoming more and more frequent. Do your bit by carrying a refillable water bottle, taking quick showers, and reusing towels. Los Angeles is also at risk of wildfires. The peak wildfire season in California is generally from July to

October when hot, dry winds are most frequent. The **Department of Forestry and Fire Protection** website has maps showing the locations of any wildfires.

Taxes and Refunds

The state-wide sales tax is 7.25 percent, though supplementary local sales taxes may be added by cities and counties. Most cities in Los Angeles County charge at least 10.25 per cent. Because none of these taxes are levied at a national level, tourists cannot claim sales tax refunds.

Accommodation

LA is vast and the traffic congestion can be bad, so it is wise to pick a hotel reasonably near the area that you intend to spend most time in. In general, anything close to the ocean will be more expensive than similar accommodations elsewhere. If you intend to arrive by car, always factor in the price of parking, which can be $45/night at some hotels.

Budget hostels and motel chains are well represented in LA. Parking and Wi-Fi are usually free.

For those visiting the Disney Resort for multiple days, it's often more sensible to relocate to a hotel in its vicinity.

A hotel with a standard year-round posted rate is rare in LA. Summers and holidays are high season. Generally on a weekend, Downtown hotels may be less expensive. Some hotels near the beach will require a minimum two-night stay.

Hotel occupancy tax is 12 per cent, and Santa Monica has a 15 per cent occupancy tax. Upscale hotels are known for charging resort fees and Wi-Fi access.

DIRECTORY

MONEY

LA Currency
ⓦ lacurrency.com

CELL PHONES AND WI-FI

AT&T
ⓦ att.com

POSTAL SERVICES

FedEx
ⓦ fedex.com

UPS
ⓦ ups.com

USPS
ⓦ usps.com

VISITOR INFORMATION

Beverly Hills Visitors' Bureau
9400 Santa Monica Blvd
☎ 310-248-1015
ⓦ lovebeverlyhills.com

Go City
ⓦ gocity.com

LA Tourism and Convention Board
ⓦ discoverlosangeles.com

Pasadena Visitors' Bureau
300 E Green St
☎ 626-795-9311
ⓦ visitpasadena.com

Santa Monica Convention and Visitors' Bureau
2427 Main St
☎ 310-393-7593
ⓦ santamonica.com

RESPONSIBLE TOURISM

Department of Forestry and Fire Protection
ⓦ fire.ca.gov

Places to Stay

PRICE CATEGORIES
For a standard, double room per night (with breakfast if included), taxes and extra charges.

$ under $150 $$ $150–350 $$$ over $350

Luxury Hotels

Beverly Wilshire
MAP J6 ▪ 9500 Wilshire Blvd ▪ 310-275-5200 ▪ www.fourseasons.com ▪ $$$
Overlooking Rodeo Drive, this dignified 1928 hotel has hosted royalty many times and featured prominently in the 1990 movie *Pretty Woman*. Luxurious extras include a chauffeured car service within a radius of 3 miles (5 km) for a fee.

The Four Seasons
MAP K5 ▪ 300 S Doheny Dr ▪ 310-273-2222 ▪ www.fourseasons.com ▪ $$$
This hotel welcomes its suite-staying guests with enormous floral arrangements. Its delights include a full-service spa and free limousine rides within a 2-mile (3-km) radius. At the Windows Lounge you may find yourself sipping cocktails next to someone famous. Children under 18 stay free with parents.

Hotel Casa del Mar
MAP A4 ▪ 1910 Ocean Way ▪ 310-581-5533 ▪ www.hotelcasadelmar.com ▪ $$$
An imposing presence overlooking Santa Monica Beach, this 1926 beach club has been restored to its original grandeur. The grand, lavish lobby is juxtaposed by the cozily decorated rooms.

Montage Laguna Beach
MAP G6 ▪ 30801 S Coast Hwy, Laguna Beach ▪ 949-715-6000 ▪ montagehotels.com/lagunabeach ▪ $$$
Atop a 50-ft (15-m) bluff with sweeping views over the Pacific Ocean, this luxury, Craftsman-style hotel is utterly gorgeous. All guestrooms have ocean views and are equipped with amenities such as deep, marble soaking tubs. Priceless early-California paintings grace the walls. Facilities offered also include a full-service spa and large swimming pool.

Hotel Oceana
MAP C2 ▪ 849 Ocean Ave ▪ 1800-777-0758 ▪ www.hoteloceanasantamonica.com ▪ $$$
One of Santa Monica's prettiest hotels, this has a fun, colorful decor that is reminiscent of the French Riviera. Many of the large suites offer guests views of the ocean.

The Peninsula Beverly Hills
MAP J6 ▪ 9882 S Santa Monica Blvd ▪ 310-551-2888 ▪ www.peninsula.com ▪ $$$
Antiques and artwork grace rooms, suites, and villas, all brimming with high-tech features, including wireless internet access and satellite TV. A personal room valet attends to your every need.

Ritz-Carlton Los Angeles
MAP S6 ▪ 900 W Olympic Blvd ▪ 213-743-8800 ▪ www.ritzcarlton.com ▪ $$$
This sleek, modern highly luxurious hotel is close to the Crypto.com Arena, the Peacock Theater, and top shopping and dining options. It shares a tower with the Marriott at LA LIVE and has a posh rooftop pool and bar on the 26th floor.

Terranea Resort
MAP D4 ▪ 100 Terranea Way ▪ 855-938-4047 ▪ www.terranea.com ▪ $$$
Located on the Palos Verdes Peninsula, with splendid views over the ocean and Catalina Island, this eco-friendly resort has 400 rooms, suites, and bungalows. Guests can while away the time at the luxury spa, with 24 treatment rooms, at the nine-hole golf course, or enjoying the gastronomic treats at the restaurant.

L'Ermitage Beverly Hills
MAP K5 ▪ 9291 Burton Way ▪ 310-278-3344 ▪ www.lermitagebeverlyhills.com ▪ $$$
Discretion is key at this sophisticated Beverly Hills hideaway with the full range of in-room high-tech amenities. Enjoy panoramic views from the rooftop pool

flanked by cabanas for extra privacy. Even pets get the royal treatment.

Waldorf Astoria Beverly Hills

MAP J6 ▪ 9850 Wilshire Blvd ▪ 800-774-1500 ▪ www.waldorfastoria beverlyhills.com ▪ $$$

The 21-story gem with Art Deco architecture was built in 2017 on the spot of the old Trader Vic's and just a few blocks from Rodeo Drive. Facilities include a chic rooftop pool, a business center, Bijan menswear boutique, and La Prairie spa.

Historic Hotels

Chateau Marmont

MAP M3 ▪ 8221 W Sunset Blvd ▪ 323-656-1010 ▪ www.chateaumarmont. com ▪ $$$

Famous recluses such as Greta Garbo holed up in this quirky French castle-style hotel, whose policy of discretion still ensures steady celebrity bookings. Revel in Hollywood lore in the cottages, bungalows, and suites.

Crystal Cove Beach Cottages

MAP G6 ▪ Crystal Cove State Park Historic District, 35 Crystal Cove, Newport Coast ▪ www. crystalcove.org/beach cottages ▪ $$

Step back in time to a quintessential California beach settlement. On the National Register of Historic Places, these 24 adorable self-catering cottages have been painstakingly restored and furnished to retain the lifestyle charm of the period between 1935

and 1955. No TVs, phones, Wi-Fi, or air-conditioning; just the sounds of the surf to lull you to sleep.

The Georgian Hotel

MAP A3 ▪ 1415 Ocean Ave ▪ 310-395-9945 ▪ www.georgianhotel. com ▪ $$$

This 1933 seaside hotel was an instant hit with the movie elite seeking to escape the Hollywood heat. Behind the Art Deco facade await guest rooms in chocolate colors, most with ocean views.

The Hollywood Roosevelt

MAP P2 ▪ 7000 Hollywood Blvd ▪ 323-466-7000 ▪ www.thehollywood roosevelt.com ▪ $$

A stone's throw away from Ovation Hollywood is this famous Hollywood hotel. While the grand lobby pays homage to the original Spanish-Mediterranean decor, most rooms have 21st-century amenities. Only the poolside cabanas retain old-fashioned flair.

Hotel Queen Mary

MAP E4 ▪ 1126 Queens Hwy ▪ 562-435-3511 ▪ www.queenmary.com ▪ $$

Stay in the roomy quarters of the *Queen Mary* ocean liner (see p73). With their wood paneling, Art Deco design and thick carpets to savor the ambience of a bygone era.

The Langham Huntington

MAP E2 ▪ 1401 S Oak Knoll Ave ▪ 626-568-3900 ▪ www.langhamhotels. com ▪ $$

This hotel is a stunning destination in itself. Take

your breakfast alfresco before lounging by the Olympic-sized, heated pool, followed by a session in the full-service spa. Enjoy afternoon high tea in the lobby lounge, then hit the tennis courts before changing for dinner at the steakhouse or at the terrace bistro – a perfect day, indeed.

The Biltmore Los Angeles

MAP U5 ▪ 506 S Grand ▪ 213-624-1011 ▪ www. millenniumhotels.com ▪ $$

A Downtown architectural landmark, the Biltmore was LA's first luxury hotel when it opened in 1923. It has hosted presidents, celebrities, and even The Beatles, who had to land their helicopter on the rooftop to avoid the fans. It is the site of several Academy Awards ceremonies, as well as a popular film location. This Beaux-Arts hotel has opulent interiors that resemble a Spanish palace. The guest rooms are comfortable.

The Beacon by Sonder

MAP A3 ▪ 1301 Ocean Ave ▪ 617-300-0956 ▪ www.sonder.com ▪ $$

Built in 1928, The Beacon has a striking Art Deco design. It features a landscaped and heated outdoor pool as well as a 24-hour fitness center but no on-site food or services. Its oceanfront Santa Monica location is one of its best features and many of the large rooms have ocean views.

Sunset Tower Hotel

MAP M3 ▪ 8358 Sunset Blvd ▪ 323-654-7100 ▪ www.sunsettowerhotel. com ▪ $$$

Once the home of John Wayne and mobster Bugsy Siegel, the Sunset Tower is a striking Art Deco tower. The former apartments are now luxuriously appointed rooms and suites, with reproductions of 1920s period furniture.

Chic and Hip Hotels

Avalon Hotel Beverly Hills

MAP K6 ▪ 9400 W Olympic Blvd ▪ 310-277-5221 ▪ www.avalon-hotel. com/beverly-hills ▪ $$

This Beverly Hills hotel has intimately lit cabanas that fringe the curvaceous pool. Rooms feature George Nelson lamps and Eames-style chairs. And don't forget – Marilyn Monroe once lived here.

Beverly Hilton

MAP J6 ▪ 9876 Wilshire Blvd ▪ 310-274-7777 ▪ www.beverlyhilton.com ▪ $$$

Famous for hosting the annual Golden Globes, this mid-century landmark is frequented by the big shots of Hollywood. It features a saltwater fish tank in the lobby, Bose music systems, and large screen plasma TVs in the rooms as well as an innovative health and fitness retreat.

Élan Hotel

MAP L5 ▪ 8435 Beverly Blvd ▪ 323-658-6663 ▪ www.elanhotel.com ▪ $$

The lobby and lounge at this stylish boutique hotel is decorated in the retro look currently in vogue.

The rooms have calming natural tones and it's close to some of the city's finest attractions. You can also order room service and pick a movie from the extensive library.

Hotel Ziggy

MAP L3 ▪ 8462 W Sunset Blvd ▪ 323-654-4600 ▪ www.hotelziggy.com ▪ $$

Located next to the Mondrian, Hotel Ziggy has a more accessible and low-key ambience. It has a relaxing saltwater pool and an onsite pizzeria.

Maison 140

MAP J6 ▪ 140 Lasky Dr ▪ 310-281-4000 ▪ www. maison140.com ▪ $$

An intimate B&B in the former villa of silent movie star Lillian Gish, Maison 140 cleverly fuses French and Asian design accents. Every room is different, but all feature patterned wallpaper and European antiques. The seductively lit Bar Noir is great for a nightcap. Excellent value for money, considering its proximity to Rodeo Drive.

Mama Shelter

MAP Q2 ▪ 6500 Selma Ave, Hollywood ▪ 323-785-6666 ▪ www.mama shelter.com ▪ $$

This stylish, offbeat hotel is within walking distance of everything in Hollywood. This is a French-based chain and the decor is color-ful, whimsical, and fun: you may just find a Darth Vader lamp in your room. iMacs substitute for TVs and radios. Don't miss the rooftop bar with views of the Hollywood Sign.

W Los Angeles

MAP C2 ▪ 930 Hilgard Ave ▪ 310-208-8765 ▪ www.marriott.com/ en-us/hotels/laxwb-w-los-angeles-west-beverly-hills ▪ $$

The chic W is full of surprises, such as the "waterfall" entrance steps and the private poolside cabanas. Suites are fully wired for connectivity, and the restaurants here are weekend hot spots. Pet-friendly rooms are available.

Freehand Los Angeles

MAP U5 ▪ 416 W 8th St ▪ 213-612-0021 ▪ www. freehandhotels.com/los-angeles ▪ $$

This hotel-hostel hybrid has turned the historic Commercial Exchange building into dozens of loft-like suites, premium hotel rooms, and shared accommodations with bunk beds. Enjoy award-winning cocktails at the rooftop poolside bar here.

Mondrian Hotel

MAP M3 ▪ 8440 Sunset Blvd ▪ 323-650-8999 ▪ www.book.ennismore. com/hotels/mondrian ▪ $$$

The rooms seem like an afterthought at hotelier Ian Schrager's celebrity outpost. Casa Madera on Sunset restaurant, the pool deck, and the hip SkyBar provide stylish hobnobbing territory.

Pendry West Hollywood

MAP M3 ▪ 8430 Sunset Blvd ▪ 310-928-9000 ▪ www.pendry.com ▪ $$$

Occupying an entire city block, this luxury hotel is

reminiscent of Hollywood's golden age with Art Deco-style architecture and spectacular artworks. The hotel hosts a culinary program headed by celebrated chef Wolfgang Puck. A glamorous rooftop pool and the famous restaurant Merois overlook the city.

Sunset Marquis Hotel & Villas

MAP L3 ▪ 1200 N Alta Loma Rd ▪ 310-657-1333 ▪ www.sunsetmarquis. com ▪ $$$

This West Hollywood hideaway is a favorite with rock'n'roll royalty such as U2. The on-site recording studio is a major draw, but so are the luxurious quarters and the Bar 1200.

Viceroy

MAP B4 ▪ 1819 Ocean Ave ▪ 310-260-7500 ▪ www.viceroyhotels andresorts.com/ santamonica ▪ $$$

The couple behind the stylish Maison 140 have created a fantasy environment that transports guests back in time to Colonial England. The decor mixes kitsch and sophistication, with a grown-up color palette of gray, bright green, and soothing cream.

Beach Hotels

Hotel Maya

MAP E4 ▪ 700 Queensway Dr ▪ 562-435-7676 ▪ www.hotelmaya longbeach.com ▪ $$

This Mayan themed waterfront hotel is set within beautiful tropical gardens. There's an open-air patio restaurant and a pool deck with fire pits and cabanas.

Beach House at Hermosa Beach

MAP A3 ▪ 1300 The Strand ▪ 310-374-3001 ▪ www.beach-house. com/hermosa-beach ▪ $$

Within earshot of the waves, this elegant getaway is the perfect antidote to stress. Just relax in front of the crackling fire in your suites.

Hotel Erwin

MAP B5 ▪ 1697 Pacific Ave ▪ 310-452-1111 ▪ www.hotelerwin.com ▪ $$

This boutique beach hotel is located close to Venice Beach and Santa Monica Pier and gives you easy access to interesting cafés and stores. Its 119 guestrooms come with the full range of amenities. The hotel has a fitness suite and rates include breakfast.

Jamaica Bay Inn

MAP B6 ▪ 4175 Admiralty Way ▪ 310-823-5333 ▪ www.jamaicabayinn. com ▪ $$

For beachfront on a budget, opt for this pleasant Marina del Rey hotel right on Mother's Beach. It is a short walk to the famous Abbot Kinney Boulevard and Venice Beach boardwalk. The sand-colored rooms have private patios or balconies.

Sea Sprite Hotel

MAP D4 ▪ 1016 The Strand ▪ 310-376-6933 ▪ No air conditioning ▪ www.seaspritehotel. com ▪ $$

Rooms in this Hermosa Beach hotel are bright and airy, but with their

location right on the beach, you probably won't spend much time inside. Larger dorms can sleep up to six.

Le Merigot

MAP B4 ▪ 1740 Ocean Ave ▪ 310-395-9700 ▪ www.lemerigothotel. com ▪ $$$

Centrally located, this Santa Monica hotel has the elegant personality of a Mediterranean mansion. Rooms are dressed in sunny, golden colors and feature patios, heavenly beds, and big desks. Bold chandeliers light up the Cézanne restaurant, where you can taste exquisite French cuisine. Excellent in-house spa.

Malibu Beach Inn

MAP A2 ▪ 22878 Pacific Coast Hwy ▪ 310-651-7777 ▪ www.malibu beachinn.com ▪ $$$

Enjoy spectacular views of the coastline from Malibu's only luxury beachfront hotel with a red-tiled Mission-style building. All rooms have gas fireplaces and balconies, some also feature a Jacuzzi. The hotel has a spa and restaurant.

Ritz-Carlton Marina del Rey

MAP B6 ▪ 4375 Admiralty Way ▪ 310-823-1700 ▪ www.ritzcarlton.com ▪ $$$

Overlooking the world's largest custom-built pleasure boat harbor, the Ritz-Carlton offers European elegance and deluxe creature comforts. Indulge in global cuisine at the stylish restaurant.

For a key to hotel price categories see p144

Shore Hotel
MAP A3 ▪ 1515 Ocean Ave ▪ 310-458-1515 ▪ www.shorehotel.com ▪ $$$
This hotel is just steps away from Santa Monica Pier. Rooms have private patios or balconies, and luxury bath products. Its Blue Plate Taco restaurant is a great place for outdoor dining and people-watching.

Shutters on the Beach
MAP A4 ▪ 1 Pico Blvd ▪ 310-458-0030 ▪ www.shuttersonthebeach.com ▪ $$$
This delightful hotel right by the sands of Santa Monica takes the beach cottage to new heights. Relax on fluffy mattresses, feel the cool ocean breeze, or watch the warm California sunlight filtering in through the shutters.

Business Hotels

DoubleTree by Hilton Hotel Los Angeles Downtown
MAP W4 ▪ 120 S Los Angeles St ▪ 213-629-1200 ▪ www.hilton.com ▪ $$
This serene Little Tokyo hotel offers a tranquil escape, especially if staying in the Japanese rooms, where you sleep on tatami mats. The spa and the beautiful third-floor Japanese gardens are great for relaxing.

Los Angeles Airport Marriott
MAP D3 ▪ 5855 W Century Blvd ▪ 310-641-5700 ▪ www.marriott.com ▪ $$
Close to LAX, this chain hotel is great for business travelers. With just over 1,000 rooms, it has a full range of conference facilities, with business and secretarial services. All rooms have wireless internet access, and high-speed connection is available at an extra cost.

Luxe Hotel Sunset Boulevard
MAP C2 ▪ 11461 Sunset Blvd ▪ 310-476-6571 ▪ www.luxesunset.com ▪ $$
A lovely property with lush landscaping, the Luxe is conveniently located right next to the 405 freeway. The spacious rooms are decorated in soothing colors. Business features include in-room tablets, complimentary Wi-Fi, and secretarial services.

The Westin Bonaventure Hotel & Suites
MAP U4 ▪ 404 S Figueroa St ▪ 800-937-8461 ▪ www.marriott.com ▪ $$
With about a dozen or so cafés and restaurants, a pool, a fitness club, shops, and a full business center, the landmark Bonaventure has more facilities than most small towns. It is well located, only 1 mile (1.6 km) from the LA Convention Center. Regular rooms are fairly small, but the office suites are well equipped.

1 Hotel West Hollywood
MAP M3 ▪ 8490 Sunset Blvd ▪ 310-424-1600 ▪ www.1hotels.com ▪ $$$
With lots of open, flexible spaces and state-of-art-technology, this luxe hotel is a popular spot for business meetings. It's conveniently located near shopping malls and Strip attractions. There's also a casual restaurant, which serves farm-to-table fare and a rooftop lounge.

Hilton Checkers Hotel
MAP U5 ▪ 535 S Grand Ave ▪ 213-624-0000 ▪ www.hilton.com ▪ $$$
An island of old-world sophistication in the fast-paced Financial District, this 1929 hotel is great for conducting business in style. Prepare for your meetings in fine leather chairs at exquisite large marble desks.

JW Marriott Los Angeles LA Live
MAP S6 ▪ 900 W Olympic Blvd ▪ 213-765-8600 ▪ www.marriott.com ▪ $$$
A short walk away from the LA Convention Center, Crypto.com Arena and LA Live, this hotel has everything you need to conduct business. The lobby is conducive to work, as are the 38 meeting rooms and the business center. After work, relax at the rooftop pool and unwind with a drink at the bar. The gym is modern and Marriott guests have access to the Ritz-Carlton spa.

Loews Hollywood Hotel
MAP P2 ▪ 1755 N Highland Ave ▪ 323-856-1200 ▪ www.loewshotels.com/hollywood-hotel ▪ $$$
This art-filled high-rise overlooks Hollywood and Highland. The suites here can accommodate small meetings. An equipped business center, PC rentals, and secretarial services are also on offer.

Omni Los Angeles Hotel at California Plaza

MAP V4 ▪ 251 S Olive St ▪ 213-617-3300 ▪ www.omnihotels.com ▪ $$$

Walk to Walt Disney Concert Hall, MOCA, and other Downtown landmarks from this modern hotel in the Financial District. Business rooms have huge desks, office equipment, and supplies.

SLS Hotel at Beverly Hills

MAP L5 ▪ 465 S La Cienega Blvd ▪ 310-247-0400 ▪ www.slshotels.com/beverlyhills ▪ $$$

Friendly and efficient staff, a business center with high-speed internet access, and meeting rooms with assets such as teleconferencing and video equipment are just some of the great perks of this Beverly Hills hotel.

Family Hotels and Motels

The Adler: A Hollywood Hotel

MAP Q2 ▪ 6141 Franklin Ave ▪ 323-464-5181 ▪ $

This modern, centrally located hotel offers relaxed rooms with character. The restaurant and tiled pool are welcome assets.

Portofino Inn & Suites

MAP F4 ▪ 1831 S Harbor Blvd ▪ 714-782-7600 ▪ www.portofinoinn anaheim.com ▪ $$

This spacious Anaheim hotel is great for wallet-watchers. The little ones will love camping out in the Family Suite bunk beds and a sofa sleeper and will get their own amenities such as TV, microwave, and fridge as well.

Cal Mar Hotel Suites

MAP A3 ▪ 220 California Ave ▪ 310-395-5555 ▪ No air conditioning ▪ www.calmarhotel.com ▪ $$

This hotel is within walking distance of Santa Monica Beach. Book an entire apartment for less money than a standard double anywhere else. Units face a landscaped pool. Located in a quiet residential street, Cal Mar is close to Santa Monica hip zones. Free parking is available.

The Garland

MAP D1 ▪ 4222 Vineland Ave, North Hollywood ▪ 818-980-8000 ▪ www.thegarland.com ▪ $$

Conveniently located close to Universal Studios, this hotel has special children's suites with bunk beds and play stations. Facilities include an outdoor pool, a gym and tennis courts.

Hotel Beverly Terrace

MAP K4 ▪ 469 North Doheny Dr, Beverly Hills ▪ www.hotelbeverly terrace.com ▪ $$

Within walking distance of Rodeo Drive and Sunset Strip, this serene hotel has a garden and pool area and provides a welcome escape from the hustle and bustle of the city. Ideally located for shopping and dining.

Kimpton Hotel Palomar

MAP C2 ▪ 10740 Wilshire Blvd ▪ 310-475-8711 ▪ www.hotelpalomar-beverlyhills.com ▪ $$

Located in Westwood village, this upscale family hotel allows you easy access to shops, restaurants, and theaters. It includes a full-service restaurant, bar, swimming pool, gym, and gift shop.

Magic Castle Hotel

MAP P2 ▪ 7025 Franklin Ave ▪ 323-851-0800 ▪ www.magiccastlehotel.com ▪ $$

Pennywise travelers love this hotel close to Hollywood action. Units vary in size but have full kitchens. Guests also enjoy access to the nearby Magic Club.

Sheraton Universal Hotel

MAP D1 ▪ 333 Universal Hollywood Dr ▪ 818-980-1212 ▪ www.marriott.com ▪ $$

Although this property can't shake off the institutional feel of a chain hotel, its location next to Universal Studios is a bonus.

Disney's Grand Californian Hotel

MAP F4 ▪ 1600 S Disneyland Dr ▪ 714-635-2300 ▪ https://disneyland.disney.go.com ▪ $$$

The price tag is a bit steep at this 751-room resort designed in richly wooded Craftsman style, but standard rooms sleep up to two adults and four kids, and it even has its own private entrance to Disney's California Adventure™ (see pp38–9) theme park.

The Pendry
MAP M3 ■ 8430 Sunset Blvd ■ 310-928-9000 ■ www.pendry.com ■ $$$

The most luxurious of all family-friendly lodgings, Pendry is a plush, stylish Hollywood hotel with 149 rooms of city and mountain views. Children get to choose a special stuffed animal upon check in and are welcomed with milk and cookies. Kid-sized robes are also available for lounging.

Budget Hotels and Hostels

Beverly Laurel Motor Hotel
MAP M4 ■ 8018 Beverly Blvd ■ 323-651-2441 ■ $$

This 1950s-style motel with a small, seasonal pool is within walking distance of the Farmers Market, Melrose Avenue, and the Beverly Center. Framed art and cheerful bedspreads adorn the rooms. The downstairs diner, Swingers (see p113), is a popular spot. Parking and Wi-Fi are chargeable.

The Rumi
MAP S5 ■ 820 S Oxford Ave ■ 310-920-0006 ■ $

This converted grand mansion in Koreatown has everything you need to sleep, bathe, and explore the city center. Most rooms are filled with bunk beds (some with privacy curtains) and each has a vintage-tiled attached bathroom. There is a strict no drinking or smoking policy.

The Hollywood Hotel
MAP D2 ■ 1160 N Vermont Ave ■ 323-746-0444 ■ www.the hollywoodhotel.com ■ $

This simple hotel is perfectly located across the street from a Metro station. Two major Hollywood tour companies pick up at their front door, offering central access to a large part of LA. All rooms have a microwave, refrigerator, and coffee maker.

Safari Inn
MAP D1 ■ 1911 W Olive Ave ■ 818-845-8586 ■ www.coast hotels.com ■ $

Easily recognized by its classic neon sign, this retro motel is nothing short of iconic. Rooms are modern with blue accents and some offer a full kitchen for convenience. Close to Universal, NBC, and Warner Bros. Studios, with specific packages offered that include studio tours and other privileges.

Sea Shore Motel
MAP B4 ■ 2637 Main St ■ 310-392-2787 ■ www. seashoremotel.com ■ $$

A Santa Monica budget abode, it is perfect for those who favor location over luxury. Only two blocks from the beach, it is on trendy Main Street with wonderful shopping and dining options.

Regency Inn
MAP D2 ■ 2378 Colorado Blvd ■ www.regencyinn losangeles.com ■ $

Located along historic Route 66 in Eagle Rock, the Regency Inn has

reliable, casual rooms, and is in close proximity to Pasadena and just a short drive from Downtown. Every room comes with a mini fridge and microwave and free parking is available on site.

Samesun Hostel
MAP P2 ■ 6820 Hollywood Blvd ■ www. samesun.com ■ $

Those traveling on a tight budget will find this friendly Hollywood hostel a good jumping-off place for their explorations. Rates include free Wi-Fi, linen and towels, storage, and access to a shared kitchen and laundry.

Short Stories Hotel
MAP M5 ■ 115 S Fairfax Ave ■ 323-937-3930 ■ www.shortstories hotels.com ■ $$

The "price is right" at this hotel opposite the Original Farmers Market and CBS, which explains its popularity with game-show contestants taping at the TV studio. The staff will organize tickets if you'd like to be part of the audience.

Hotel Angeleno
MAP C2 ■ 170 N Church Lane ■ 310-476-6411 ■ www.hotelangeleno. com ■ $$

The rooms in the cylindrical Hotel Angeleno are self-catering with mini-fridges and floor-to-ceiling windows overlooking the historic neighborhood. With an outdoor pool, fitness center, restaurant, cocktail lounge, and no-tipping policy, it is solid value for money.

Inn at Venice Beach

MAP B6 ▪ 327 Washington Blvd ▪ 310-821-2557 ▪ www.innat venicebeach.com ▪ $$
The beach beckons outside this small hotel on the border of Venice and Marina del Rey. Rooms offer moderate comforts and a cheerful decor.

B&Bs

Elaine's Hollywood Bed & Breakfast

MAP N2 ▪ 1616 N Sierra Bonita ▪ 323-850-0766 ▪ No credit cards ▪ www.elaineshollywoodbedand breakfast.com ▪ $
This beautifully restored 1910 bungalow has two rooms available and is located in a quiet neighborhood. Elaine's is a perfect base for exploring Hollywood and its gracious hosts will help you plan your outings.

Malibu Bella Vista

MAP A2 ▪ 25786 Piuma Rd ▪ 818-645-1159 ▪ www.malibubella vista.com ▪ $
Nestled in Malibu Canyon, the ranch-style Bella Vista is ideally located just minutes from the beach and good hiking trails. Spa facilities are available and the excellent Saddle Peak Lodge gourmet restaurant is close.

Beachrunners' Inn

MAP E4 ▪ 231 Kennebec Ave ▪ 562-856-0202 ▪ www.beachrunners inn.com ▪ $
This restored 1913 Craftsman home is within walking distance from the Long Beach coastline. Choose from six modern bedrooms and enjoy an elaborate continental breakfast with your stay.

Bissell House

MAP E1 ▪ 201 Orange Grove Ave ▪ 626-441-3535 ▪ www.bissell house.com ▪ $$
This stately 1887 Victorian home has a prestigious address on Pasadena's famed "Millionaire's Row." A sedate, grown-up atmosphere reigns in the elegant public areas and all eight cozy rooms. There is no disabled access here.

Channel Road Inn

MAP C2 ▪ 219 W Channel Rd ▪ 310-459-1920 ▪ www.channelroad inn.com ▪ $$$
A Neo-Colonial home built in 1915, it is clad in wooden shingles and sits on the northern edge of Santa Monica. Each room has different perks such as fireplaces, lovely four-poster beds, patios, soaking tubs, or a view.

Dockside Boat & Bed

MAP E4 ▪ 316 E Shoreline Dr ▪ 562-436-3111 ▪ Limited air-conditioning ▪ www.boatandbed.com ▪ $$
A unique getaway, this floating B&B has on offer a fully equipped sailboat, motor yacht, and even a Chinese junk. Boats are moored in Long Beach's Rainbow Harbor; enjoy views of the Queen Mary.

Garden Cottage B&B

MAP M5 ▪ 8318 W 4th St ▪ 323-653-5616 ▪ www.gardencottagela.com ▪ $$
Ideal for families on a moderate budget, this friendly B&B offers three rooms in an elegant 1929 house, with a shared garden, a formal dining room, and a kitchen, and a private cottage. The B&B is located close to The Grove shopping center and the popular Farmer's Market at 3rd and Fairfax

Venice Beach House

MAP A6 ▪ 15 30th Ave ▪ 310-823-1966 ▪ www.venicebeachhouse.com ▪ $$$
Built in 1911 by relatives of Venice founder Abbot Kinney (see p122), this delightful inn is a witness to Venice history. A quiet oasis, it allows you to retreat to the comforts of cozy, antique-filled rooms after a busy day at the beach or in town.

Inn at Playa del Rey

MAP B7 ▪ 435 Culver Blvd ▪ 310-574-1920 ▪ www.innatplayadelrey.com ▪ $$$
Modern and breezy, this B&B is close to the ocean and Marina del Rey, and overlooks the Ballona Wetlands Ecological Reserve. Some rooms have Jacuzzis and fireplaces. Close to LAX airport, the B&B also offers free parking and bicycle rental.

Banning House Lodge

MAP C6 ▪ 1 W Banning House Rd ▪ 310-510-7331 ▪ www.visitcatalina island.com ▪ $$
Set on the west end of Catalina Island, Banning House is perched on a hill above Two Harbors village. A former hunting lodge, built in 1910, it has been restored as a B&B with evening wine and cheese socials on offer for guests too.

For a key to hotel price categories see p144

General Index

Page numbers in **bold** refer to main entries.

Acknowledgments

This edition updated by

Contributor Sarah Bennett
Senior Editors Dipika Dasgupta, Alison McGill
Senior Art Editor Stuti Tiwari
Project Editors Sarah Allen, Anuroop Sanwalia
Project Art Editor Ankita Sharma
Editor Mark Silas
Assistant Editors Tavleen Kaur, Vineet Singh
Picture Research Administrator Vagisha Pushp
Picture Research Manager Taiyaba Khatoon
Publishing Assistant Simona Velikova
Jacket Designer Ankita Sharma
Jacket Picture Researcher Kate Hockenhull
Cartographer Ashif
Cartography Manager Suresh Kumar
Senior DTP Designer Tanveer Zaidi
Senior Production Editor Jason Little
Production Controller Kariss Ainsworth
Managing Editors Shikha Kulkarni, Beverly Smart, Hollie Teague
Senior Managing Art Editor Priyanka Thakur
Art Director Maxine Pedliham
Publishing Director Georgina Dee

DK would like to thank the following for their contribution to the previous editions:
Catherine Gerber, Helen Peters, Clare Peel, Caroline Pattern

20br, 20cla, 21tl, 22tr, 22clb, 23tc, 107tr.

Polo Lounge: 119clb.

Providence: Noe Montes 66c.

Shutterstock: 117clb; Paul C Barranco 3tl, 74–75; Walter Cicchetti 118t; Gerry Matthews 23bl; Rolando Otero 69cl; Hayk_Shalunts 111br; StandbildCA 51tr; Stock Connection 47clb.

Robert Harding Picture Library: Eye Ubiquitous 28cl; Gavin Hellier 4crb; H. & D. Zielske 4cra.

San Antonio Winery: 85t, 89cla.

Sawdust Art Festival: 132cla.

SkyBar: 112cla.

SuperStock: All Canada Photos / Robert Postma 129cra; Citizen of the Planet 34br, 49crb.

TCL Chinese Theatre: 2tl, 8–9, 63cl.

El Tepeyac Cafe é: 89cb.

Hammer Museum: 116cl.

Universal Studios Hollywood: 7br, 32br, 32–3, 33tl; Zack Lipp 33cr.

Viper Room: 15tl.

Water Grill: 66t.

Cover

Front and spine: **4Corners:** Susanne Kremer.

Back: **123RF.com:** Fabio Formaggio crb, tr; **4Corners:** Susanne Kremer b; **Getty Images / iStock:** LPETTET tl, Art Wager cla.

Pull Out Map Cover

4Corners: Susanne Kremer.

All other images © Dorling Kindersley
For further information see:
www.dkimages.com

Penguin Random House

First edition 2004

First published in Great Britain by Dorling Kindersley Limited, DK, One Embassy Gardens, 8 Viaduct Gardens, London SW11 7BW, UK

The authorised representative in the EEA is Dorling Kindersley Verlag GmbH. Arnulfstr. 124, 80636 Munich, Germany

Published in the United States by DK Publishing, 1745 Broadway, 20th Floor, New York, NY 10019, USA

Copyright © 2004, 2024 Dorling Kindersley Limited
A Penguin Random House Company

23 24 25 26 10 9 8 7 6 5 4 3 2 1

The publishers cannot accept responsibility for any consequences arising from the use of this book, nor for any material on third party websites, and cannot guarantee that any website address in this book will be a suitable source of travel information.

A CIP catalog record is available from the British Library.

A catalog record for this book is available from the Library of Congress.

ISSN 1479-344X
ISBN 978 0 2416 6480 3

Printed and bound in Malaysia

www.dk.com

*As a guide to abbreviations in visitor information blocks: **Adm** = admission charge; **D** = dinner.*

MIX
Paper | Supporting responsible forestry
FSC™ C018179

This book was made with Forest Stewardship Council™ certified paper – one small step in DK's commitment to a sustainable future.
For more information go to www.dk.com/our-green-pledge